BBC MUS

C000264433

TCHAIKOVSKY

BBC MUSIC GUIDES

Bach Cantatas J. A. WESTRUP
Bach Organ Music PETER WILLIAMS
Bartók Orchestral Music JOHN MCCABE
Beethoven Concertos and Overtures ROGER FISKE
Beethoven Piano Sonatas DENIS MATTHEWS
Beethoven String Quartets BASIL LAM
Beethoven Symphonies ROBERT SIMPSON
Berlioz Orchestral Music HUGH MACDONALD
Brahms Chamber Music IVOR KEYS
Brahms Piano Music DENIS MATTHEWS
Brahms Orchestral Music JOHN HORTON
Brahms Songs ERIC SAMS
Bruckner Symphonies PHILIP BARFORD
Debussy Orchestral Music DAVID COX
Debussy Piano Music FRANK DAWES
Dvořák Symphonies and Concertos ROBERT LAYTON
Elgar Orchestral Music MICHAEL KENNEDY
Handel Concertos STANLEY SADIE
Haydn String Quartets ROSEMARY HUGHES
Haydn Symphonies H. C. ROBBINS LANDON
Mahler Symphonies and Songs PHILIP BARFORD
Mendelssohn Chamber Music JOHN HORTON
Mendelssohn Orchestral Music PHILIP RADCLIFFE
Monteverdi Madrigals DENIS ARNOLD
Mozart Chamber Music A. HYATT KING
Mozart Piano Concertos PHILIP RADCLIFFE
Mozart Serenades and Divertimenti ERIK SMITH
Mozart Wind and String Concertos A. HYATT KING
Rachmaninov Orchestral Music PATRICK PIGGOTT
Ravel Orchestral Music LAURENCE DAVIES
Schoenberg Chamber Music ARNOLD WHITTALL
Schubert Chamber Music J. A. WESTRUP
Schubert Piano Sonatas PHILIP RADCLIFFE
Schubert Songs MAURICE J. E. BROWN
Schubert Symphonies MAURICE J. E. BROWN
Schumann Orchestral Music HANS GAL
Schumann Piano Music JOAN CHISSELL
Schumann Songs ASTRA DESMOND
Shostakovich Symphonies HUGH OTTAWAY
Tchaikovsky Symphonies and Concertos JOHN WARRACK
The Trio Sonata CHRISTOPHER HOGWOOD
Vaughan Williams Symphonies HUGH OTTAWAY
Vivaldi MICHAEL TALBOT

BBC MUSIC GUIDES

Tchaikovsky Ballet Music

JOHN WARRACK

BRITISH BROADCASTING CORPORATION

Contents

Introduction	5
Swan Lake	15
The Sleeping Beauty	32
The Nutcracker	54

Author's Note

I should like to acknowledge help and advice given me by Dr Roger Fiske, Mr Noël Goodwin and Dr Henry Orlov. I am also grateful to Mme Xenia Davydova and Mme Galina von Meck; as grandchildren of Tchaikovsky's sister Alexandra Ilyichna Davydova, they provided me with useful family information, and Mme Davydova was unfailingly generous in answering queries over material in her care at the Tchaikovsky House-Museum at Klin.

Dates are normally given in New Style; the Old Style dating is added only in cases of possible confusion, e.g. in references to the dates on which articles appeared in periodicals.

Published by the
British Broadcasting Corporation
35 Marylebone High Street
London W1M 4AA

ISBN 0 563 12860 7

First published 1979

Typeset in Great Britain by Eta Services (Typesetters) Ltd., Beccles, Suffolk
Printed in England by Whitstable Litho Ltd., Whitstable, Kent

Introduction

I completely fail to understand what you call ballet music and why you won't accept it. Do you mean by ballet music any cheerful and dance-like tune? But in that case you can't accept most of Beethoven's symphonies, in which it can be found at every turn. Are you trying to tell me that the trio of my scherzo is written in the style of Minkus, Gerber and Pugni? This seems to me unfair. I totally fail to understand how the expression *ballet music* can be something *disapproving*!

Tchaikovsky's retort to Taneyev, who had incautiously observed that there was a flavour of ballet music in the Fourth Symphony, came from the heart. He loved music for dancing, and as early as October 1870 he had planned what he described to his brother Modest as 'a huge four-act score' for a ballet on *Cinderella*. Nothing came of this project, which he seems to have abandoned at a fairly early stage, and none of the music is known to have survived. But his devotion to the idea of the dance as a stimulus to music lasted all his life; and the vehemence of his remarks to Taneyev, his favourite pupil and a friend who usually had great licence in criticising his music, shows how deeply he felt about music that was rooted in the dance and about its possibilities for serious artistic use.

Cesare Pugni, Yuly Gerber and Ludwig Minkus represented a tradition of official ballet music whose feebleness Tchaikovsky was the first to acknowledge. Not only was their talent negligible: it was required to be negligible. Their 'vulgar concoctions', as Tchaikovsky described them in a letter, were expected to do no more than furnish unobtrusive aural décor and rhythmic support as a background against which the dancers could be put through their paces. It was, moreover, décor that was infinitely disposable and replaceable: no fewer than eighteen composers were finally represented in the music of *The Little Humpbacked Horse,* a score nominally by the unfortunate Pugni whom Mussorgsky described to Balakirev as 'a musical Scythian'. The situation was not unusual, for few composers had the talent or the resolve to stand up to ballet masters whose interest was principally in the decorative. The attempts made by more serious-minded choreographers to involve music in the action usually foundered on the inability of composers, in a youthful Russian musical tradition, to find ways of sustaining and developing dance music as a vehicle for anything but the most conventional action and emotion. There were those who tried. Ivan Valberkh (or Waldberg), a ballet master who graduated from the Theatre School in 1786, was able to graft on to eighteenth-century conventions of prettiness some feeling for realism and for the life of ordinary people: he was a self-educated man with many literary friends, and would have been responsive to the current enthusiasm for Rousseau. Anything portraying life was categorised as a 'ballet of morals', and Valberkh (who in his diary criticised the Paris ballet for its superficiality) was up to a point successful in introducing real feelings into his works: at any rate, his patriotic *ballets d'action* of 1812 sent men straight from the theatre to the recruiting office. However, associated as he was with composers unable to charge his ideas with music of sufficient power, Valberkh could not make much progress in the direction of a truly organic composition of dance and music; and though he and the composer Alexey Titov did make some attempt to weave dance into the action, as in *Blanca, or Marriage out of Revenge* (1803), he was also apt to fall back on sets of dances as divertissements attached to weddings or other festive occasions.

An attempt at involving music and dance more integrally came from a rather different direction with Charles Didelot, a gifted man of the theatre whose particular talent was for skilful, sensational shows. Pushkin, on whose *Captive of the Caucasus* Didelot wrote a ballet, described him in *Eugene Onegin* as 'winged with fame', adding in a note that his ballets were 'filled with lively imagination and extraordinary charm'. For *Raoul de Créquis* (1819), Didelot had the services of Caterino Cavos (and his pupil Timofey Zhuchkovsky); and in planning the scenario he anticipated later practice by working out for them a careful sequence of scenes in the action and the length and nature of the musical numbers to be fitted into it. However, the intention seems to have been to keep the music clearly in its place rather than to devise for it expressive opportunities: Didelot always regarded music as the servant of the choreography. Comparable attempts at a more unified artistic form were made by Jules Perrot, who arrived in St Petersburg in 1848 and worked on the *danse d'action* in which the aim was for dance both to arise from the action and to further it.

Perrot and even Didelot were found too advanced by the Directors of the Imperial Theatres in St Petersburg, for whom ballet meant no more than diversion. The arguments about the function of the arts that had begun to divide Russians by the middle of the century left ballet largely untouched; as the most purely decorative of the theatrical arts, it was clearly part of the pretty, the elegant and the fantastic which have always been facets of Russian life. Some of the realist literary critics, headed by Vissarion Belinsky, had admired the ballerina Ekaterina Sankovskaya for the sense of human truthfulness she had brought into ballet; but their absorption in the 'grave questions', in the need to form an art that would be truly connected to life, soon led them to dismiss ballet as a frivolity for the amusement of 'starched dandies and youthful old men', as one bitter attack described it. Naturally the effect was to isolate ballet still further, to exaggerate its tendency to meaningless décor and self-regarding virtuosity. The arrival in Russia of Arthur Saint-Léon served only to confirm this. In him the Directorate was satisfied that they had found a man who would keep ballet in its role of entertainment to the aristocracy and the Imperial Family, and who would above all keep his own place without demanding artistic independence. Though himself able to compose, he never gave music a serious role in his ballets: these were essentially a reversion to the divertissement, ingeniously distributed across a full-length ballet, against which Perrot had reacted. Though immediately successful, Saint-Léon's ballet *The Hump-Backed Horse* seems in its original form to have been scarcely more than an elaborate spectacle, dressed out with tableaux and centring on a *divertissement* of dances by various of the nationalities indigenous to Greater Russia. Its novel use of a popular Russian fairy tale as subject acted as a potent attraction, though in fact it remained wholly fixed in the conventions which Saint-Léon had re-established. Not surprisingly, the work aroused deep distaste among the intelligentsia, for whom the veneer of Russian-ness was visibly artificial; and this was a view more generally shared in Moscow, where Saint-Léon's ingenuity in dressing his dancers fantastically and in devising ever more amusing new patterns for them was less appreciated. As Tolstoy was to observe in *War and Peace,* it was substance that prevailed in Moscow life, form in St Petersburg.

Like Saint-Léon, Marius Petipa had studied music, but he too began by giving it a comparatively minor role in ballet. Yet his work, with all its faults, moved the art decisively forwards to the point at which dance and narrative were to join more expressively with music. In his concern for dramatic content, Petipa was a follower of Perrot. He was also capable of lapses into triviality in the Saint-Léon tradition; yet though he never eradicated the tendency to pointless prettiness which marks his work, his gifts as a choreographer included the ability to handle narrative and crowd scenes, to give his divertissements greater relevance, to construct dance sequences with a variety that contained elements of real dramatic development. He retained to the end a delight in using extravagant and sometimes absurd props, as in the first of his *ballets à grand spectacle, Pharaoh's Daughter* (1862), in which a 'grand ballabile des cariatides animées' required eighteen pairs of dancers to carry on their heads baskets of flowers out of which emerged thirty-six small children. However, Petipa also had ambitions for enlarging the expressive range of his art, and these were bound to include the giving of greater importance to music. His large-scale dance compositions were based on musical, even symphonic principles, with solos developing from a simple idea proposed by the *corps de ballet*, other groups acting and reacting in contrast, and much else. It seems likely that Petipa's own musical training, working on his choreographic art, led him to feel the need for a more substantial musical contribution, rather than simply his liking for music making him interested in employing better composers. The tendencies that were to be developed in his work with Tchaikovsky already showed in 1870 over his projected collaboration with Alexander Serov. A memorandum sent to Serov requested him to 'compose melodious music, as this is the most important requisite for the production of dances'; and he further requested that Serov should attend rehearsals so as to expound the detail of his music and make any necessary cuts – a stipulation Petipa might well have regretted with that sharp-tongued critic. Seven years later, as Tchaikovsky produced his *Swan Lake* score for Julius Reisinger's mediocre choreography, Petipa was attempting to devise a symphonic ballet, *La Bayadère*, with music by the inadequate Minkus. In a tradition that was, as Tchaikovsky's friend Hermann Laroche wrote, 'identified with musical farce', even Petipa proved slow to recognise that the musical strength he sought was to be found in Tchaikovsky's unique combination of gifts.

From his earliest years, Tchaikovsky had been drawn to music for dancing. 'As far as the Russian element in my music is concerned,' he told Nadezhda von Meck, 'that is, the relationship between the national songs and my melodies and harmonies, this exists because I grew up in the backwoods, from earliest childhood saturated with the indescribable beauty of the characteristic traits of Russian folk music, because I passionately love their Russian element in all its manifestations.' In the autumn of 1869 he completed, for his publisher Pyotr Jürgenson, a collection of arrangements for piano duet, *Fifty Russian Folksongs*; and though he had only collected one of these himself (the others being taken from the collections of Villebois and Balakirev), it was an idiom he knew and loved deeply from the inside. Among the 'manifestations' which he appreciated was the use of folksong in the traditional Russian folk polyphony, the *podgolosok* which he recreates in several of his operas, including at the beginning of *Eugene Onegin*; and no less important was the association of song with dance which immediately follows in this scene. The ancient chain or circle dance, still popular in Eastern Europe as the *kalamatianos* of Greece or the *kolo* of Jugoslavia, was as the Russian *khorovod* performed to the accompaniment of singing; indeed, the etymology of the word is *khor* = choir, *vodit'* = to lead. This close association gave Russian dance from its earliest times a particular expressive quality. The medieval troupes of entertainers known as *skomorokhi*, who make their appearance in various Russian operas, were musicians as well as dancers, jugglers, acrobats and in general figures of misrule, 'the Devil's offspring'. They were adept at the *skakat*, a term that probably covered the most acrobatic aspect of their performances and included vigorous dancing: the word only occurs in Old Slavonic chronicles, with negative connotations (*besovskiye skakaniya* meant 'devilish leaping'). They were also masters of the *plyaska*, the term for Russian folk dances which might be vigorous but could be slow, graceful, even lyrical. Certainly *plyaska,* the Old Slavonic word for 'dance', implied an invention with steps and movements arranged spontaneously; *tanets*, from the word for 'dance' used in some form in most Western European languages, was only introduced as the normal Russian word under Peter the Great, and originally meant something more measured and composed. In his incidental music for Ostrovsky's *The Snow Maiden* (1873), Tchaikovsky included both a number entitled 'Dances and birds' chorus' and a 'Skomorokhs' *plyaska*'; and as early as 1865 he had had one of his first public successes with a set of *Characteristic Dances* that were given their first performance in Pavlovsk Park by none other than Johann Strauss. These dances were later incorporated into his first opera *The Voyevoda*, a work which was later abandoned after the salvaging of some of its better music for later use (in *1812* and *Swan Lake*). From his admired Glinka, who had experienced his own troubles with choreographers, Tchaikovsky had learnt the effect of dance music of different kinds within the structure and narrative of an opera; and he includes a *plyaska* along with other dances in every one of his operas up to *The Queen of Spades*, where the dictates of the plot require the pastoral dance in the Act 2 entertainment to be of a formal, quasi-eighteenth-century nature. *Yolanta*, his last opera, has no room for dancing in the brief plot, and in any case was designed to appear in the same bill as *The Nutcracker*.

However, these dance episodes were invariably placed in opera as special events, attached to weddings or other festivities at which the dancing was there for its own sake, outside the plot and observed by the singers in the same terms as it was by the audience. Tchaikovsky, with his attraction to French opera and the traditions of the Paris Opéra, saw no reason to question this as a statutory feature. It was in his symphonies and concertos that he showed interest in making use of the characteristics of Russian folk song and dance as a structural force. From Glinka, and from *Kamarinskaya* in particular, he had learnt the expressive power of developing a tune by varied repetition, both in harmony, in figuration and not least in orchestration: the finale of his Second Symphony, based on the technique, was hailed by Stasov as 'one of the most important creations of the Russian school'. More elaborately, he discovered ways of using a folk dance to generate an entire movement by variation and by combination with other musical elements arising from it, as with the finale of the First Piano Concerto; and his life-long fondness for beginning a symphonic work with a slow introduction that was later embodied in some way in the movement originally arose from his successful handling of the folk theme which opens the Second Symphony. Development in the manner of the German symphonic tradition was never Tchaikovsky's strongest point; but his closeness to Russian folk music, and his feeling for its structural and harmonic implications as well as its melodic flavour, opened up for him a whole range of ingenious and attractive ways of constructing large symphonic movements. In his sonata form movements, there can sometimes be a sense of strain in his attempts to effect a reconciliation between the conflicting demands of systematic development and the complete 'lyrical idea' to which he attached prime importance, and which is of its nature not susceptible to much in the way of progressive modification. But the enrichment of his technique which this brought about enabled him to give to extended dance movements, based on a 'lyrical idea', a symphonic quality which was at that time completely unknown in Russia. The composition of *Swan Lake* dates from 1875–6, between the first group of three symphonies and the Fourth Symphony with which Tchaikovsky achieved symphonic greatness.

Not surprisingly, contemporary audiences found Tchaikovsky's ballets, in particular *The Sleeping Beauty*, 'too symphonic' – a complaint Tchaikovsky would not have minded since the same charge was levelled by Paris critics against his beloved Delibes. His natural Russian orientation towards Latin rather than Teutonic art took extreme form when he told Nadezhda von Meck that he preferred Delibes to either Brahms or Wagner; and he later added that *Swan Lake* was 'poor stuff compared to *Sylvia*'. But he was answering her enquiries about his natural tastes, rather than expressing critical judgement; and his attraction to Delibes derived from the recognition that here was an example upon which his own invention could feed. In fact, *Sylvia* was not performed until three months after *Swan Lake*, and Tchaikovsky did not come to know *Coppélia* until 1878. He had by then solved the most important of his problems about constructing a full-length ballet that should also be a dance drama in music, and much of his pleasure in Delibes must have lain in the discovery that here was another artist who had found a way of combining short characteristic dances, virtuoso solos and ensembles with longer scenes into a structure that was at once colourful and cohesive.

One important means by which Tchaikovsky gave expressive unity to his ballet scores was his subtle and far-reaching use of tonality. With *Swan Lake* in particular, this was more than a matter of connecting dances by natural key-sequence or startling contrast: a basic tonality (in the case of *Swan Lake,* B) could be identified with the central dramatic idea, and the substance of the action related by key to this. With it firmly established as the centre of a key-complex, the placing of an entire act in an unrelated key could become an expressive symbol of the drama taking an unexpected or threatening course; while within these long-range key-patterns, the introduction of divertissements in unrelated keys (yet held together within themselves by keeping to their own key-pattern) would serve to indicate both musically and dramatically that they were incidental to the main progress of the drama. The divertissements, not only satisfying the need for giving opportunities to secondary dancers or small ensembles, could in addition provide dramatic contrast, also introducing sequences of exotic, national or otherwise colourful dances in neat, self-contained numbers; for the narrative and lyrical or dramatic passages central to the plot, more substantial thematic development, perhaps making use of motive, was appropriate. By such means, the condition was created for a dance drama that could include diversion while reserving the true expressive weight for the larger narrative and lyrical sections.

Tchaikovsky's gift with the divertissements has remained supreme in the history of ballet music, as is witnessed by the undimmed popularity of the *Nutcracker Suite* (a popularity which dates from before the complete ballet was heard). His acute ear for melody enabled him to touch on the essence of various styles or national dances with uncanny accuracy, giving them thereby a new freshness and point; and confident of his abilities in this quarter, he was also able to give such characteristic dances a more realistic position in the drama, while maintaining a clear distinction between them and the variations which (as with those for the fairies at Aurora's christening in *The Sleeping Beauty*) are functionally involved with the drama. Among his contributions to the genre was his ear for orchestral colour, which was intrinsic to his invention: as he told Nadezhda von Meck, 'the musical idea appears already coloured by a certain scoring'. His discovery of the celesta in Paris led him to include it in *The Nutcracker* not merely for its own effect, greatly concerned though he was that the secret instrument should not be revealed prematurely to his musical rivals; he was able to devise for it in the Sugar-Plum Fairy's dance a piece of music that is for ever identified with its delicate chime, exquisitely poised against a reduced group of eighteen pizzicato strings and the sensuous softness of the bass clarinet. The refinement, concentration and sweetness are dramatically appropriate, while at the same time the music contains the sense of physical movement that is an essential part of his ballet style. The orchestration is not a separate and distinct element in his invention: by colour and contrast, by its vividness and its forcefulness, it can give rhythms that are available to any composer a potency and an infectious energy that are unique to Tchaikovsky. He drew upon many dance rhythms: from the distinguished history of French classical dance as with minuet, gavotte and farandole; from his own Russian heritage; from exotic lands as with the bolero and the tarantella, or in a piece of imaginative identification as with the Chinese and Arabian dances in *The Nutcracker* suggested by the idea of tea and coffee. He used polka, mazurka, polonaise, sarabande, galop, and above all the dance rhythm to which he gave a new range of character, waltz. His first waltz dates from 1854, when he was fourteen and just beginning to compose; a suite of eighteen pieces written in the last year of his life includes a *Valse à cinqtemps*. It was a dance that held a perennial delight for him, one which he was able to elevate to symphonic status and to which he brought a lyrical intensity that made it a cornerstone of his ballet scores, adaptable to moments of lyrical intensity, to diversion, or to the sweeping up of all the characters in a General Waltz.

To all the ingredients of ballet Tchaikovsky was able to give point and character, conferring greater musical distinction on the diversions, turning the traditional dancers' Adagio from something sentimental and inert into a lyrical episode of emotional substance, and especially developing symphonic sections of narrative into a position of novel importance. He was careful to keep stylistically within the bounds appropriate for magic and fairy-tale, sensing that a major part of the music's role was to justify the connection between a children's story and the sophisticated artistic technique in which it was expressed: to this extent, the ballet exists substantially in the music. However much he resented Taneyev's remarks deploring a balletic element in his Fourth Symphony, he maintained in his mind a clear distinction between the expressive aims of ballet, opera and symphonic music. Opera and symphony were for him an expression of life, in the case of the last three symphonies of the bitterness and frustration of his own life and the 'Fate' which he believed to be hanging over it. Ballet was for him associated with the decorative, and with a grace and prettiness that afforded a relief from life. These qualities might legitimately be composed into the Fourth Symphony, with its programme as described to Nadezhda von Meck of 'turning away from reality and plunging into dreams', of 'some bright, gracious human form' appearing as a vision, of 'dreams completely enveloping the soul' before the reverie is harshly interrupted by reality. Such visions were part of his longing to seek an escape from the deepening unhappiness of his life, tormented as he was by his homosexuality and craving the peace and fulfilment of the steady female love that seemed to lie beyond his grasp. The art of the ballet offered an elegant, graceful and brilliant escape in which reality played a minimal role: there is a rare touch of Tchaikovsky's own inmost feelings in the Finale to *Swan Lake*, when the passion that overcomes the music reflects his belief that love is to be found only against the most malevolent opposition from inhuman forces, and may even then be denied fulfilment. He did not again put so much of his own anguish into dance music. Regarding prettiness, *le joli,* as a legitimate aspect of music, as he wrote in connexion with his beloved *Carmen,* he reserved this side of his gifts for the art he regarded as associated with a blissful escape into a never-never land of childhood and fantasy, in which wicked fairies can be routed, love awoken from its sleep by a kiss, in which the battles fought are between dolls and mice and the reward for being brave a visit to the Kingdom of Sweets. To be able to present emotions in terms of *le joli* was for him a happy relief from troubling reality, a re-entry into the innocence of childhood and the acutely remembered warmth of his family circle and his lost mother. It gave him the greatest satisfaction to be able to apply his talents to such an art. In so doing, he raised fairy-tale ballet to its highest expressive capacity, giving it a warmth and a colour that were to epitomise the genre, setting a standard for later composers and even for Prokofiev in his *Cinderella* and Britten in his *Prince of the Pagodas*. Moreover, he took ballet forward to the point at which a new expressive gesture was demanded. Seventeen years after Tchaikovsky's death, Stravinsky wrote for Diaghilev his *Firebird,* a fairytale ballet in the Tchaikovsky tradition and the first step in Stravinsky's merging of the art of movement with music of unprecedented power. Stravinsky, who paid his homage to Tchaikovsky by using his piano music and songs for *The Fairy's Kiss,* was the first to acknowledge the influence upon him of Tchaikovsky's 'wonderful talent'; and in the open letter he wrote to Diaghilev on the occasion of the 1921 revival of *The Sleeping Beauty* he insisted that

> Tchaikovsky's music, which does not appear specifically Russian to everybody, is often more profoundly Russian than music which has long since been awarded the facile label of Muscovite picturesqueness. This music is quite as Russian as Pushkin's verse or Glinka's song. While not specifically cultivating in his art the 'soul of the Russian peasant', Tchaikovsky drew *unconsciously* from the true, popular sources of our race.

Swan Lake

Spending the summer of 1871 at his sister Alexandra Davydova's house at Kamenka, Tchaikovsky amused himself by writing for her children a one-act domestic ballet called *Swan Lake*. Virtually nothing is known of this entertainment, in which the composer's brother Modest took the part of the Prince; but it must have passed into family lore, for Yury Lvovich Davydov, who was born in 1876 and lived on at Klin until 1965, claimed to have remembered that the music included a theme which he 'immediately recognised' when he first heard the 'swan' melody in the mature ballet. The initiative for this 3-act ballet seems to have come from the inspector of repertory of the Imperial Theatres, Vladimir Begichev. The author of various plays, he also held court in a kind of salon. 'In his flat,' wrote Karl Waltz in *65 Years in the Theatre* (Leningrad, 1928), 'I met Turgenev, Dargomyzhsky, Serov, Ostrovsky, Rubinstein, Tchaikovsky and many others.' No single member of the circle laid claim to authorship of the scenario, and the supposition is that they worked something out in discussion, perhaps on the basis of what Tchaikovsky described of the family entertainment, but also drawing upon well-known fairy tales. The most likely source here was Johann Musäus's *Volksmärchen der Deutschen,* published in 1782–6 and familiar to educated Russian children in the German original; the most likely authors are Begichev himself and the dancer Vassily Geltser.

At about the end of May 1875, Tchaikovsky received the commission for a full-length ballet on *Swan Lake* from the Directors of the Moscow theatre. Later, on 22 October, he was to tell Rimsky-Korsakov that 'I accepted the work, partly because I want the money, but also because I have long had the wish to try my hand at this kind of music'. The money can actually have weighed less with him than his interest in the task: it amounted to 800 rubles (then about £85). By 26 August he was writing to Taneyev to say, 'I have sketched out (in project) two acts of *The Lake of Swans*', having, according to the memoirs of the critic Nikolay Kashkin, begun to study in detail other ballet scores. Work progressed well: some numbers of Act 1 were ready for rehearsal in the Theatre School at the beginning of April, and the score was finished at Glebovo on 10 April. The first performance, in Moscow on 4 March 1877, was tepidly received. Preparations had gone badly, with the orchestra complaining about the unprecedented difficulty of the score and, it seems, finding little clarification from their conductor, Stepan Ryabov: Modest described him as 'a semi-amateur who had never been faced with so complicated a score'. The dancers also rebelled, unable to cope with a work that provided them with more than a string of elegant or virtuoso numbers. The décor was feeble, as contemporary drawings show, and was parcelled out between three designers in a manner suggesting at best haste and more probably a rehash of previous work. Acts 1 and 3 went to two obscure men named Shangin and Gropius; acts 2 and 4 were in the hands of Karl Waltz, a machinist and décor artist who had come to the Bolshoy in 1861 to work on the electrical fittings, and had contributed pyrotechnic effects to various productions. The first Odette/Odile, Pelageia Karpakova, was a poor mime, and not really of ballerina standard: she is said to have been given the role because she enjoyed influential patronage. The senior ballerina who soon replaced her, Anna Sobeshchanskaya, was more sensitive, but had at thirty-four begun to pass her prime. Siegfried was danced by Stanislav Gillert, Rotbart by Sergey Sokolov, the Princess by Olga Nikolayeva, Benno by Sergey Nikitin, and Wolfgang by Wilhelm Wanner. One of the original reviews complained that the choreographer, Julius Reisinger, merely showed 'remarkable skill in arranging gymnastic exercises'; while the *Theatrical Gazette* for 22 February (6 March) spoke of 'a few successful moments . . . but in general the music of the new ballet is rather monotonous, dull . . . interesting probably only to musicians'. It was not long before insertions and deletions began to maim the original concept, some of the numbers being cut as 'too difficult', and other music by Pugni being added. In his *Reminiscences of P. I. Tchaikovsky*, Nikolay Kashkin recalled:

Swan Lake had a success, if not a great one certainly a success, and it was performed for many years until the décor was worn out and never renewed. Not
only was the décor ragged; the music suffered more and more until nearly a
third was changed for music from other ballets – not necessarily good ones.

Though there was a revival in 1882, the history of *Swan Lake* as a
successful ballet really begins with the choreography by Marius
Petipa and Lev Ivanov. Act 2 was staged in 1894 (after Tchaikovsky's death), and the first complete performance of this version
took place as a Benefit for Pierina Legnani, with Pavel Gerdt, at
the Maryinsky Theatre in St Petersburg on 27 January 1895; the
conductor was Riccardo Drigo. There is evidence that work on
this began in Tchaikovsky's lifetime; but not long after the
première he was already viewing his score with his usual melancholy self-doubt. In comparing *Swan Lake* unfavourably to *Sylvia*
when writing to Nadezhda von Meck on 8 December 1877, he
added, 'Nothing during the past few years has charmed me so
greatly as this ballet of Delibes, and *Carmen*.'

To appreciate the superiority of *Swan Lake* to the mild if
delightful *Sylvia,* it is necessary to consider the score as Tchaikovsky
composed it for dance action. However, there are problems in
deciding what his final intentions were. The first published
Jürgenson full score of 1895 does not represent the original 1877
performance; and Petipa's extensive alterations for the 1895 revival
(which include the shortening of Act 1 and the building up of the
character of Odile) are not included. It seems probable that the
Jürgenson score, and the similar score in the Complete Collected
Edition (1957), both based on the composer's autograph, represent
the version used in 1882. Certainly that September Tchaikovsky
wrote to Jürgenson from Kamenka asking for the full score and
piano reduction so that he could make an orchestral suite. Later
vicissitudes, such as the insertion of music by lesser composers and
the alteration of the plot, belong to theatrical rather than musical
history. For instance, Petipa's transposition of the Pas de deux from
Act 1 (No. 5) to Act 3, where it became known as 'The Black
Swan', for the 1895 production, principally brought about that
conflict of musical and choreographic interest which has bedevilled
most Western productions since. Notable attempts to return to
Tchaikovsky's original sequence have been made in productions
by Vladimir Bourmeister (1953), Jack Carter (Buenos Aires 1963,
later London Festival Ballet), and Peter Darrell (a centenary pro-

duction for Scottish Ballet, 1977). Tchaikovsky's structure is musically strong and coherent, well designed to articulate the dance drama and to include suitable occasions for diversion while concentrating the expression on the tragic story.

The basis of this is a carefully organised key system. The fundamental key of the tragedy is B: Act 1 opens in B minor and closes in B major; Act 2 opens and closes in B minor; and the conclusion to Act 4 and the entire work moves beyond B major onto five bars of a unison B. Within this, the main action tends to be connected to A, together with its dominant, E, and subdominant, D. In Act 3, as the deception deepens and the forces of evil gain ascendancy, the pull is towards flatter keys: the act begins in C (after an introduction in G, moving, as was Tchaikovsky's habit, onto the tonic as the curtain rises); and the flat pull drags the last number from its basic C major into a close on F. Act 4 moves from A minor to the concluding B. These are no more than tendencies, and as the work progressed Tchaikovsky felt able to move more freely; but they provide general tonal centres for the essential elements in his plot. The most important part of the action can thus be given a sense of musical progress and coherence, while the divertissements can normally be shown as outside the dramatic plot by being placed also outside the tonal plot. They naturally attract the lightest, most immediately appealing side of Tchaikovsky's invention, while for the longer scenes of drama and emotion he reserved the manner which was to confuse the untutored listeners of the day by its symphonic organisation. The contrasts imposed by dance action, with its need to move between different soloists or groups, were no disadvantage to a composer who claimed 'the lyrical idea' as the basis of his inspiration; and the Glinka-inspired technique of varied accompaniment was also to be the motive force in certain numbers; but it was his growing ability to sustain large musical structures by drawing on different methods of development that gave *Swan Lake* a new range and depth in ballet music. Motive plays some part in this, as does the use of certain recurrent devices such as rising scales to indicate tension or falling scales (often chromatic) to represent the threats of Fate; but the handling of the various techniques of development shows a new confidence and mastery in his music. Only a few weeks after the première, Tchaikovsky began the first of his three great symphonies about Fate, the Fourth in F minor.

ACT I

Introduction

Instead of what was in his day a conventionally lively overture to settle late-comers into their seats, Tchaikovsky provides a short (62-bar) outline of the emotional content of the drama. The opening melody is the first Swan theme:

Ex.1

It is answered on clarinet; then the theme passes to cellos, under characteristic wind and horn triplet decorations, with the answer given to violins over one of the descending 'Fate' basses that mark the whole invention:

Development of (*x*) leads to an Allegro ma non troppo and a powerful climax, out of which comes a passionate statement of Ex. 1 over a long pedal A. The movement is a succinct introduction not only to the content but to some of the most important techniques of the ballet.

No. 1: Scene

The scene represents part of a magnificent park: a castle is visible in the distance. An elegant bridge crosses a stream. Prince Siegfried and his friends are seated at tables drinking.

From the continued pedal A, bustling string figures generate expectancy in a series of rising sequences that on curtain-rise take the music onto the tonic, D: the vigorous chordal theme for full orchestra stands for the rejoicing at the Prince's birthday, and is underpinned by a rising scale. It is characteristic of Tchaikovsky's sense of economy that the bustling figures also prove to be part of the main thematic invention.

A crowd of peasants come to congratulate the prince. His tutor Wolfgang invites them to entertain the prince with their dances; they agree. The prince orders wine for them. Servants carry out his orders. The women are given flowers and ribbons.

The second of these two quotations from the score (which normally only includes stray indications of the scenario) provides the occasion for a central episode in B minor, beginning with oboes and clarinet over droning bassoon bagpipe-fifths, and quickly leading to a return to the relative major with the opening music of the scene, exactly repeated.

No. 2: Waltz

By setting this waltz, one of the most famous in history, in the 'central' key of A major, Tchaikovsky confirms its role as a dance of action rather than divertissement: it is organically connected to the birthday celebrations that impose on the reluctant Prince the need to choose a wife and abandon his irresponsible merry-making, and it is danced by the entire corps de ballet. The point is reinforced by the vigorous, active nature of the music, in contrast to many of Tchaikovsky's more purely decorative waltzes. It is constructed with two trio sections, in F sharp minor and D minor respectively, the latter including a prominent cornet solo.

No. 3: Scene

A messenger comes to announce the arrival of the Prince's mother. The servants put everything in order. The tutor assumes a serious air. The Princess enters and enjoins marriage on her son: the merry-making is premature. She leaves, and the Prince declares that this means an end to their carefree life. Benno consoles him: they resume their places and the dance begins again.

The narration begins with an A major representation of the carefree young people (in an A minor key signature), interrupted by a fanfare for the Princess that picks up their pattering triplets and turns them into a more formidable figure: this is the horns' first entry in the piece, and it is in the contrast between their handling of an insistent triplet figure and the triplets of the young people that the key moment of the piece exists. A lyrical theme on strings leads to a return of the opening music as the Princess leaves, and the 'merry-making' triplets lead, by way of a brief fugato on the triplets, to an abbreviated restatement of the festive music of No. 1.

No. 4: Pas de trois

The first of two divertissements for the peasants in the Act is cast in six sections, its key-complex of B flat placing it firmly outside the main action. Though brief, the pieces have a self-contained sequence and key-balance, as well as musical contrast. I: Intrada (B flat: 6/8): a soaring melody for woodwind and strings over harp. II: Andante sostenuto (G minor: 3/4): a duet canon between oboe and bassoon, with a short central episode, suggesting a contrast between male and female dancers. III: Allegro semplice (E flat: 2/4): a lively polka initiated by the clarinet and developing into a presto flute theme on semiquavers that brings the dance to an end on a suggestion of the original festive music. IV: Moderato (C minor: 6/8): a powerfully scored, vigorous movement suggesting a male dance. V: Allegro (F major: 2/4): by contrast, very lightly scored until the final climax. VI: Coda; allegro vivace (B flat: 4/4): a more substantially developed piece to round the diversion off.

No. 5: Pas de deux

The second divertissement of the Act, for two of the merry-makers, consists basically of two waltzes, separated by an elaborate movement for violin solo, and concluded with a coda. I: Tempo di valse: a brief waltz somewhat in the vein of the waltz of No. 2. II: Andante-Allegro: based on the Hungarian *csárdás* form of *lassú-friss* (slow-fast), this is quite an elaborate solo for violin, with cadenza-like figuration in the central section, that leads into a vigorous dance. III: Tempo di valse: a short waltz based on a dialogue between cornet with violins and two clarinets. IV: Coda; Allegro molto vivace: a vigorous conclusion, with much percussion and emphatic use of pedal points in a very simple harmonic structure on G major.

No. 6: Pas d'action

The tutor, drunk, dances and by his awkwardness causes general amusement.

Tchaikovsky ingeniously builds an Andantino-Allegro movement out of this episode by first giving Wolfgang a dignified tune:

Ex.3

As the old man becomes drunk, he begins spinning faster and faster to the phrase marked (*x*), and this, after his collapse on a loud chord, becomes a general dance on a new theme deriving from it:

Ex.4

No. 7: Pantomime

It is growing dark. One of the guests proposes that the last dance shall be with their goblets in their hands.

A 16-bar introduction, leading to:

No. 8: Goblet Dance

A long, brilliant polonaise, firmly tethered to E major though with certain hints of the gathering darkness and menace in the appearances of the descending chromatic scale and in episodes swerving onto flat keys (e.g. E flat minor).

No. 9: *Finale*

A flight of swans appears in the air. Benno suggests a hunt: the Prince agrees, but they decide to leave behind the now incapable Wolfgang.

Richly scored with harp arpeggios and tremolo strings, there appears a new 'swan-maiden' theme: this is the tune that probably featured in the children's ballet.

Ex.5

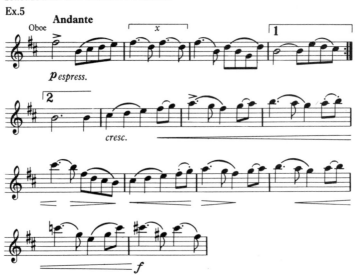

This is developed into a powerful B major climax whose strong descending scale figures end the Act on an ominous note.

ACT 2

No. 10: *Scene*

In a mountain landscape at dusk, a lake is shimmering in the moonlight. The ruins of a temple are visible. Siegfried watches the swans swimming on the lake: he is joined by his friends.

Tchaikovsky originally intended this as an entr'acte (and marked it thus in his autograph); subsequently he revised it as a scenic tableau, though the only direction surviving in the score is at bar 13, 'The swans are swimming on the lake'. Ex. 5 is developed, chiefly by selection and increasingly impassioned orchestration of its phrases.

No. 11: Scene

The hunting party gather and take aim at the swans, who are transformed into beautiful girls. Their leader asks, 'Why do you persecute me?' She tells him that she is the Princess Odette, and that they have all been bewitched by her evil stepmother and Rotbart: by day they are swans, but now that it is night they revert to human form. Only a marriage vow contracted in the face of death can break the spell. Rotbart appears in the guise of an owl, and threatens Siegfried.

This, the most elaborately narrative section of the score so far, is based firstly on a vigorous dotted note theme for the hunting party and Siegfried, and secondly (after a suggestion of the characteristic falling thirds of (*x*) in Ex. 5 for the glimpse of the swan-maiden) a graceful new oboe melody as Odette reveals herself and asks why he persecutes her. Her narrative is to a new Allegro vivo theme that occupies the rest of the movement, apart from the violent brass and wind triplet figure that accompanies the appearance of Rotbart as an owl.

No. 12: Scene

A flight of swans appears overhead, and circle around Siegfried. Odette tells them to desist: 'He is good'. Siegfried throws away his gun. The scenario suggests that Siegfried, already in love with Odette, begs her to attend his betrothal ball tomorrow, when he will choose her; but she reminds him of the threat of Rotbart and her stepmother.

In this second scene of narrative and action, Tchaikovsky varies his technique by developing symphonically a single little figure:

Ex.6

until Odette intervenes with another oboe phrase; this is answered by an orchestral tutti, and the scene ends with a delicate passage for woodwind, marked in the score with Odette's words, 'Be calm, knight.'

No. 13: Dance of the Swans

Though this number takes the place of a divertissement in an act that otherwise consists of four action scenes, it is a functional part of the plot and the lyrical centre of the act as Siegfried and Odette declare their love; consequently it is more closely organised than the previous divertissements. It takes the form of a Rondo, with a sweeping A major waltz (strings answered by brief woodwind phrases) as the subject. The first episode (E major) is a Moderato assai in 6/8 for Odette that ends with a faster section. After a reprise of the Waltz (A major), the second episode is an Allegro Moderato in F sharp minor to a theme on chattering oboes over bassoon fifths. This is the number taken over by Petipa and Ivanov as the Dance of the Little Swans: it should not be confused with the Dances of the Young Swans that is No. 27 in Act 4, and was thus entitled by Tchaikovsky. There follows not a return to the Waltz, but a substantial *pas d'action*. Originally forming part of the love duet for Undine and Hulbrandt in Tchaikovsky's discarded opera *Undine*, it here takes the form of a harp solo introducing a lyrical statement of the theme on violin answered, after a quicker section, with the theme on cello with violin counter-melody: this leads in turn to an Allegro conclusion. The movement satisfies the need for a Grand Adagio in the conventions of contemporary Russian ballet; but its musical weight and emotional substance, as well as its skilful placing in the plot, give it a quality that would have been novel to audiences reared on the tradition of the Adagio as a vapid and merely decorative display of a dancer's line. As it ends in E flat, the reprise of the Waltz is now in A flat, and is, moreover, interrupted with more vigorous chords that serve to project the music into a Coda (E major, 6/8) that takes the form of a vigorous general dance.

No. 14: Scene

Dawn breaks. Odette and her friends withdraw into the temple, to reappear on the lake as swans.

A complete restatement of the B minor No. 10.

ACT 3

No. 15: Allegro giusto

The ball-room of the castle. Wolfgang orders the servants to admit the guests, and they are followed by the Princess, Siegfried and their retinue of pages and dwarfs.

A vigorous introduction, establishing the key of C at curtain rise after 16 bars on a dominant pedal: the characteristic descending chromatic bass here has no fateful significance. A middle section accompanies the entry of the Princess and Siegfried.

No. 16: Dance of the corps de ballet and the dwarfs

The Master of Ceremonies orders the revels to commence.

Again, a 16-bar introduction on the dominant (C, from the previous number), and at the cadence reflecting the descending chromatic scale, establishes the main key of F for the Allegro vivo dance. In contrast to this straightforward, conventionally scored piece for full orchestra, the trio for the dwarfs, in the relative minor, is a gracefully grotesque section for oboe, clarinet, and bassoon over horn fifths, answered by a pizzicato passage.

No. 17: Scene: Guests' Arrival and Waltz

New guests are announced, including an old Count with his wife and daughter, who begins to dance with one of the knights. Six eligible Princesses arrive with their parents and take their places.

There is a double introduction to the Waltz proper: fanfares lead by way of a figure played by clarinets in thirds to its first abbreviated statement; renewed fanfares similarly lead to a second, varied version of the waltz; and finally the same pattern precipitates the closing and fully extended waltz. It is in nature (including in its orchestration) more pompous than the relaxed Act 1 waltz.

No. 18: Scene

The Princess asks her son which of the visiting Princesses is his choice, but he refuses to answer. Baron Rotbart enters with Odile in the guise of Odette. Siegfried welcomes her and the ball recommences.

After a short introduction, the fanfares from No. 17 announce Rotbart and Odile: the opening music is in fact a modification into 4/4 of the waltz, and the nature of the descending opening figure is made clear when, at the presentation of Odile, a powerful descending scale on bassoons, brass, and lower strings indicates the Fate motive openly. The harsh statement of Ex. 5 suggests the outward resemblance of Odile to Odette while revealing her true nature to the listener.

No. 19: Pas de six

Variations for the visiting Princesses.

The movement consists of an Intrada, five variations and a Coda (though the second variation was omitted in the numbering in the autograph). The Intrada is marked by 'formal' dotted-note figures and skirling woodwind thirds. Variation I (Allegro, 2/4) is in ABA form, with the opening clarinet tune taken over by flute after a central tutti: possibly it was intended for Odile. Variation II (Andante con moto, 2/4) begins with a dialogue between oboes and bassoons in thirds and sixths, turning after a central tutti to a new figure on clarinet and flute. Variation III (Moderato, 6/8) is a short number basically for strings with woodwind decorations. Variation IV (Allegro, 4/4) is more vigorous and extended, based on an energetic triplet figure, and leading to Variation V (Moderato, 4/4: a harp cadenza; then Allegro semplice, 2/4), an oboe solo joined by clarinet and moving into a lively più mosso tutti. The Coda (Allegro molto, 2/4) is a very powerful, emphatically rhythmic dance scored for full orchestra. It will be seen that again Tchaikovsky has made the occasion for divertissement play a proper structural part in the design of the act: the music is well contrasted, providing a demonstration of the different characters of the princesses and acting as a formally self-contained group of numbers in a key-progression F–B flat–G minor–E flat–C minor–F minor–A flat.

Added number

For the first of the added numbers required in 1877, Tchaikovsky wrote a *pas de deux* for Siegfried and Odile in the form of an Introduction (Moderato – Andante), Variation I (Allegro moderato), Variation II (Allegro) and Coda (Allegro molto vivace). However, only the second variation was orchestrated by the composer: the remainder of what is not the most distinguished part of the score was orchestrated for a production at the Stanislavsky-Nemirovich-Danchenko Theatre in Moscow in 1953 by Vissarion Shebalin, perhaps rather too creamily though the use of the cornet in the middle section of the Coda is a characteristic *Swan Lake* touch.

There follows a suite of national dances, presented by guests from different lands. As part of his carefully established key-plot,

Tchaikovsky makes these seem outside the dramatic plot by setting them in a series of sharp keys, as well as giving them a tuneful exuberance and a relish of exotic colour that is in no way connected to the musical drama.

No. 20: Hungarian Dance

A piece cast in the *csárdás* pattern of *lassú-friss*: a brief A major introduction leads to the A minor slow section, followed by the vigorous A major fast section.

At this point, Tchaikovsky was obliged by Julius Reisinger to add a Russian Dance for Pelageia Karpakova, the directorate feeling that such a piece of national colour would please. It is a regrettable insertion; for though Tchaikovsky liked it well enough to make a piano reduction and include it in his set of pieces, Op. 40 (No. 10), it is not among his most distinguished inventions, and its repetition of the fast-slow pattern is too close in manner to the preceding Hungarian Dance. However, he fitted it ingeniously into his key pattern for the suite by setting it in A minor, thus relating it both to the preceding and succeeding dances, but also giving it a relationship to the main key of the Act, C, and thus making it seem less distant than the other 'lands'.

No. 21: Spanish Dance

In every way, the Spanish Dance, with its F sharp minor opening (the relative minor of A major), provides a better contrast to the Hungarian Dance. It is also one of the best in the sequence, contrasting the vigorous bolero opening, all clicking castanets and impassioned dotted noted scalic figures against the basic beat, with a fine F sharp major section that sets a surging tune essentially in 2/4 against the steady bolero 3/4. It ends with the obligatory frenzied stamping, più mosso.

No. 22: Neapolitan Dance

A perfunctory four bars swerve the key from F sharp to D for an Andantino in which a cornet delivers itself of a serenade tune of a vulgarity that would not be out of place in the Italian Capriccio; the second part is the inevitable Tarantella.

No. 23: Mazurka

An energetic dance, scored for the full orchestra with a witty central section for clarinets and oboes, danced by soloists and corps de ballet.

No. 24: Scene

The Princess is pleased that Siegfried accepts Odile. He announces that he will marry her, and invites her to dance with him. He kisses her hand. The Princess and Rotbart join their hands. The scene darkens: Rotbart turns into an owl and flies screeching from the hall. Odette is glimpsed, as a white swan, through the castle archway; the Princess sinks to the ground, and Siegfried rushes out into the night.

Required to compress the most dramatic action of the ballet into a short space, Tchaikovsky has recourse to the motivic methods that must have been largely responsible for the initial complaints about the work's symphonic nature. The 4/4 version of the Waltz, No. 17, introduces Siegfried's invitation to Odile to dance with him, and the waltz is repeated in shortened form. Their betrothal is conducted to a brief, very tense passage out of which emerges the harsh statement of Ex. 5 as in No. 18. A violent brass figure disposes of Rotbart, and as Siegfried rushes out, the fiercely scored, abrupt ending gives the crisis a sense of sudden horror in ironic contrast to the easy diversion of the national dances.

ACT 4

No. 25: Entr'acte

The music is taken over from Tchaikovsky's early opera *The Voyevoda* and the duet for Maria and Olena in Act 2, scene 2 ('Tikho luna vzoidet': 'Silently the moon is rising'): the Entr'acte to Act 3 of the opera is virtually the same as this Entr'acte, and opens with a phrase that is repeated between harp cadenzas, in various abbreviations and forms and in various scorings.

Ex.7 **Moderato**

No. 26: Scene

Odette's friends await her by the lake, unable to understand where she has gone.

Ex. 7 is developed into a new form, its fragmentation further reflecting the disarray among Odette's companions:

Ex.8

The movement, a touching and forlorn piece, ends with a cadence figure (*y*) derived from Ex. 7:

Ex.9

No. 27: Dances of the Young Swans

The melancholy, obsessive theme of the dance takes up the cadence figure (*y*) for a characteristic feature of its theme (later also making prominent use of (*z*)).

Ex.10

This is also, however, another derivation from *The Voyevoda* (Bastryukov's Act 1 aria):

Ex.11

No. 28: Scene

Odette, heartbroken at Siegfried's apparent desertion of her, rushes into the arms of her companions. A storm rises, and Siegfried struggles through it to find her.

A busy semiquaver figure, beginning on a figure derived from (y) in Exx. 7, 9 and 10 whose first three notes have dominated the end of No. 27, is now built up to a climax; and out of it emerges a slower passage for Odette's narration. The storm generates its force in busy triplet figuration, with rising chromatics and sequences of sevenths in traditional Romantic fashion, over long held pedals that move down at each restatement from D through C sharp until they reach the fundamental key of the work, B.

There is, throughout these four numbers, a close thematic argument and a symphonic development unprecedented in ballet music. Even the Dances of the Young Swans, a number occupying the position of divertissement in the Act, is far from being mere diversion. In its gentle, obsessive, swaying rhythm it reflects the distress of the trapped, bewitched swans, and the subtle use of thematic material that marks these four scenes gives the dance a vital expressive role in the tragedy. Moreover, the means of development employed by Tchaikovsky is based on allusive repetition rather than progressive argument. In this it is essentially Russian, relating to the tendency of Russian folk music to proceed by modification rather than development or contrast. It also looks back to methods of sustaining the structure through varied accompaniment, harmony and orchestration as developed by Glinka; but further, it looks forward to the use of repeated and subtly modified figures that was to characterise the work of Stravinsky. The movement is virtually a slow *khorovod* in the manner Stravinsky was to use for the *Ronde des princesses* in *The Firebird*.

No. 29: Final scene

The Prince begs Odette's forgiveness, but she dies of grief in his arms. He casts her coronet on the waters, which rise and engulf the lovers. As the scene calms, the swans are seen gliding across the calm surface of the lake.

The opening music of the scene again derives from *The Voyevoda*, the long-awaited meeting of the lovers in No. 2 of Scene 3. Ex. 5 returns, very agitated over syncopated accompaniment, and eventually achieves a grand apotheosis in the major. But the triumph of love over the malevolent forces of Fate has something of the hollow ring of over-assertion which marks the comparable major-key triumph at the end of the Fifth Symphony. For Tchaikovsky, the truer ending is the enigmatic close on a long held open unison B, neither major nor minor.

The Sleeping Beauty

So skilfully designed is the music of *Swan Lake* that had the work found the audience it deserved in 1877, Tchaikovsky's career, and with it the history of ballet music, might have been significantly different. Especially in the last act, where the situation of love frustrated by a malevolent Fate touched acutely on his own predicament, Tchaikovsky achieved a formal strength that placed him in the position to make his next ballet a more substantial dance drama; yet it was this very act which suffered the most severe mutilations, Drigo's changes including the cutting of Nos. 26 and 27 and the beginning of the storm, and the substitution of two dances to music taken from the Op. 72 Piano Pieces of 1893. Other changes had meanwhile altered the musical balance, committing to 'tradition' a distortion of a very carefully planned musical design. More than a decade was to elapse before Tchaikovsky returned to ballet music, years which saw his disastrous marriage and the beginning of his friendship with Nadezhda von Meck; while the major works of the period include *Eugene Onegin* and three more new operas, and among symphonic works *Manfred* and the Fourth and Fifth Symphonies. In a life that had grown increasingly sombre and burdened with the unhappiness of his homosexuality, opera and particularly symphonic music became the more important means of expression; while ballet music became more and more associated with a dream world, unreal and pretty.

Yet Tchaikovsky was never one to underrate the claims of *le joli*, as he had emphasised in his praise of *Carmen*; and he was quick to respond when an approach for a new ballet came from the Director of the Imperial Theatres, Ivan Vsevolozhsky. Born in 1835, Vsevolozhsky was by profession originally a diplomat, serving for some years in Paris before being appointed to the Imperial Theatres in 1881. He was a man of wide culture and intelligence, gifted as an artist and as a writer (he had two plays produced in 1890 and 1898), and an organiser of efficiency and vision. Finding that the standard of ballet had sunk to a low level, with virtuosity doing duty for expression among the dancers and with costumes and décor that were merely perfunctory, he initiated a series of searching reforms. He set up a rehearsal hall, organised a teaching syllabus, founded the *Annual of the Imperial Theatres* (which ran from 1890 to 1915, and is an invaluable source of information), and formed an advisory panel for the production of ballets consisting of the scenario writer, the composer, the designer, the choreographer and the stage manager. The intention was to ensure a collaboration between all those involved in the creation of a ballet, so as to achieve a homogeneous style. He was, however, disposed towards the *féeries* then popular as a reflection of Parisian taste, such as the notorious *The Magic Pills* in which the disapproving Petipa was obliged to invent sequences of dances for dominoes and playing cards. *The Sleeping Beauty* was clearly intended to be another but more artistic *féerie*.

On 25 May 1888, Vsevolozhsky wrote to Tchaikovsky, remarking in the course of his letter,

It would be very nice, incidentally, to write a ballet. I've planned a libretto on *La Belle au bois dormant* to Perrault's tale. I want the *mis en scène* to be in the style of Louis XIV. Here one could work up a musical fantasia and write melodies in the spirit of Lully, Bach, Rameau etc. If you like the idea, why don't you write the music? In the last act there would have to be a quadrille from all Perrault's tales – here one could have Puss-in-Boots, Hop-o'-my-Thumb, Cinderella and Bluebeard, etc.

Some mishap seems to have occurred about the dispatch of the promised synopsis, for on 1 September Tchaikovsky was replying to a letter from Vsevolozhsky saying that he had not received it, but adding, 'I am very interested in the subject.' A few days later he did receive a copy, and telling his brother Modest that it was 'superb' he also wrote to Vsevolozhsky to say, 'I want to tell you at once that it's impossible to describe how charmed and captivated I am. It suits me perfectly, and I couldn't want anything better than to write music for it.'

Tchaikovsky's interest in the subject seems to have gone back further than he admitted, or has hitherto been widely known. Two years previously, in November 1886, he had held discussions with Vsevolozhsky on the possibility of writing a ballet, but the subjects then proposed, *Salammbô* and *Undine*, did not attract him. However, he seized on *The Sleeping Beauty* with alacrity, perhaps the more so since he had, as with *Swan Lake*, once before mounted a little entertainment at Kamenka for the children of his sister Alexandra. On that occasion, Tatyana played the Princess, another sister was the Prince; the part of a Cupid, standing over the Sleeping Beauty, was played by a third sister, Anna, then aged only three and too young to do more. (It was she who later married Nadezhda von Meck's son Nikolay: she twice described this entertainment to her daughter Galina, who gave the information to the present writer.) This would date the entertainment as 1867, Anna having been born in 1864; yet her memory, as with that of her brother Yury's over *Swan Lake*, is of being told that Tchaikovsky provided music which later found its way into the mature *Sleeping Beauty*.

In November, Tchaikovsky held a conference with the Directors and with Petipa, and agreement was reached on draft outline of the scenario. After the difficulties over *Swan Lake* and the need to match particular artistic demands, and wishing moreover to fit closely into the more unified project being planned by Vsevolozhsky, he requested a detailed scenario from Petipa. Part of this arrived in December, the remainder in the New Year. It consisted of an elaborately detailed 'Programme' for a 'fantastic ballet in five acts', set out (in French) using black ink for the scenario and red ink for the musical instructions, in numbered sequence. Outlined for the composer were not only the plot and the division into ensembles, solo dances and so forth, but often meticulous musical instructions. Petipa gave Tchaikovsky, for example, detailed instructions for Aurora's entrance, as what was then No. 9 of Act 1:

(9) Aurora's Entrance. She runs out accompanied by her attendants, who carry bouquets and garlands. The four princes are struck with her beauty. Each of them craves her favour and love. But Aurora dances among her suitors, showing no preference.

(9) *From 16 to 24 bars, leading to another tempo. At Aurora's entrance, perky, coquettish 3/4, 32 bars, ending with 16 bars 6/8 forte.*

What Tchaikovsky eventually wrote was eighteen bars of introduction; then a new tempo and thirty-one bars of music for Aurora's entrance that could well be described as perky and coquettish; and finally twenty-two bars of 6/8, fortissimo. Like many ballet and film composers since his day, he seems to have found this kind of detailed demand a stimulus rather than a hindrance to his invention, a genuine collaboration rather than submission to another artist. Petipa in turn presented ideas to the costume designer, Vsevolozhsky himself, for instance sketching in his note book neat designs for the fairy godmothers Violante and Candide, each with two attendant little fairies, and notes (also in French) explaining his intentions. Vsevolozhsky's own costume drawings are, like many of their kind, lively and colourful, but represent detailed indications to the wardrobe mistress rather than drawings of great artistic worth. But it was he who controlled the enterprise, from its conception through the choice and supervision of its creators and artists to the organisation of the production itself.

As soon as he had received the first batch of the scenario from Petipa, Tchaikovsky set to work. He finished the sketch by 7 June (N.S.) 1889, noting on the score, 'Finished sketches 26 May at 8 o'clock in the evening. Thank God!'; and he added that he reckoned it had occupied about forty working days. The orchestration was more of a problem. He wrote to Nadezhda von Meck on 6 August:

It seems to me, my dear friend, that the music of this ballet will be one of my best creations. The subject is so poetic, so grateful for music, that I have worked on it with enthusiasm and written it with the warmth and enthusiasm upon which the worth of a composition always depends. The orchestration is causing me, as I think I already wrote to you, more trouble than it used to, and the work is going much more slowly, but perhaps this is all for the best.

The last chord was written, he told his friend Yulia Shpazhinskaya, on 1 September. A telegram from Vsevolozhsky received on 27 December 1889 (8 January 1890) announced, 'First performance ballet 3 [15] January, dress rehearsal Tuesday 2 [14], we hold general rehearsal Saturday 30 [11 January].' The Tsar was present at the dress rehearsal, but to Tchaikovsky's rage merely observed 'Very charming'. '"*Ochen' milo*"!!!!!', he repeated furiously in his diary. 'His Majesty treated me in a very offhand manner. God be with him.'

The first performance, on the following night, had been given all the preparation Vsevolozhsky could lavish on it. The conductor was Riccardo Drigo, who for all his subsequent vandalism of Tchaikovsky's ballet music was an efficient musician experienced in his craft. The décor, despite Vsevolozhsky's reform of the old abuse of having sets painted by different artists, was shared out between Levot for the Prologue; Mikhail Bocharov (a company designer with a special talent for exteriors and *paysages*) and Ivan Andreyev for Act 1; Bocharov for the exterior and panorama of Act 2 and K. M. Ivanov for the castle interior; and the veteran Matvey Shishkov produced a lovely formal garden panorama for Act 3. Possibly the sets were influenced by Gustave Doré's wonderful illustrations to Perrault, which had appeared in 1807;

certainly Vsevolozhsky's costumes were clearly based on those used in Cicéri's famous Paris Opéra production of Hérold's *La Belle au bois dormant,* which was first performed in 1829 and lasted in the repertory of the Opéra until 1840. Princess Aurora was danced by Carlotta Brianza, newly arrived in St Petersburg from Italy as a guest artist and aged only twenty-two, and said to be initially rather angular and brittle in her style: photographs of her in the role do not suggest a very fairy-like presence. Prince Désiré was danced by Pavel Gerdt, then past his forty-fourth birthday but still the outstanding male dancer of his day. A distinguished array of dancers filled the smaller parts, with Felix Kshesinsky as King Florestan, Enrico Cecchetti as the Blue Bird and also Carabosse, and Petipa's daughter Maria as the Lilac Fairy: really a character dancer, whose large stature prevented her from dancing classical roles, she had made a speciality of Good Fairies, and the limitations of her choreography are shown by a photograph of her in the role in which she is wearing high-heeled shoes. (Rudolf Nureyev, himself Leningrad-trained, reverted to this concept of the Lilac Fairy when he first mounted his own production at La Scala, Milan, in 1966, later repeated for the National Ballet of Canada (1972) and London Festival Ballet (1975).)

Despite all the care lavished on it, the first performance was not a great success with public or critics. The low standing ballet had as an art in intellectual circles was reflected in much of the comment, including from the greatest contemporary music critic, Vladimir Stasov. Always a very hesitant admirer of Tchaikovsky, he dismissed Vsevolozhsky as an 'insipid Frenchman' and in a letter to Nikolay Findeisen regretted the fashion for 'china dolls' and Tchaikovsky's music for them. The *St Petersburg Gazette* repeated the old charge against *Swan Lake* that, 'In the theatre, the music seemed symphonic, melancholy.' However, Tchaikovsky's loyal friend Hermann Laroche wrote in the *Moscow Gazette* of his pleasure that a composer of Tchaikovsky's gifts, one whom he firmly hailed as 'one of the leading melodists of our time', had lavished this talent upon ballet. The critic of *The New Age*, Mikhail Ivanov, a former composition pupil of Tchaikovsky, also came to the defence: 'Tchaikovsky's music for *The Sleeping Beauty* has provoked reproofs in several reviews for its unnecessarily symphonic qualities, reproofs which have already been levelled at previous ballets ... This tendency is understandable, because

36

Tchaikovsky cannot abandon the resources of his art for the sake of the prejudices of earlier choreographers. These are noticeable still more in *The Sleeping Beauty*, where the subject demands an intense application of symphonic style.' But all the merit of the score, the defence of sympathetic critics, and the increasing enthusiasm of the dancers could not prevent the usual distortions and mutilations overtaking the work. Even in modern times, and despite the Diaghilev revival of 1921 which called forth Stravinsky's eloquent defence and his orchestration of several numbers omitted by Tchaikovsky, stagings of separate acts (such as Act 3 as *Aurora's Wedding*) or special versions of the work have been common. The work's fame in the West dates from the Vic-Wells revival of 1939, made possible by the presence in England of Nikolay Sergeyev (who had danced in Russian productions of the 1890s); and since 1946 there have been over 500 performances of the complete ballet at Covent Garden alone.

Ivanov's counter to the reproving reviews is well judged. *The Sleeping Beauty* is a 'symphonic' score principally in the sense that instead of providing the conventional row of short, disjunct dances, it engages properly with a strong, flexible dramatic and choreographic design; and also in that it makes prominent use of the conflicting themes of the wicked Fairy Carabosse and the good Lilac Fairy. Each act, including the Prologue, is based on a narrative opening and close (apart from the token final Apotheosis); each includes scenes where dance forms a natural part of the plot; each is also planned to include at its centre a set of solo variations with only a token connection to the story. Such a scheme provides a plot to give coherence to a full evening's entertainment, company numbers and numbers in which a characteristic dance grows out of the plot so that attention is concentrated in turn on dances and on action, and solo numbers in which to pure dance there is added the element of personal virtuosity. The formula is similar to that of *Swan Lake*, but it is more elaborately detailed, with greater attention given to balance and contrast rather than to thematic references or to a large-scale tonal plan. Possibly Tchaikovsky now felt able to dispense with these disciplines: it is common for a composer tackling a new medium to feel the need for a very secure structure, then in subsequent works in the medium being able, out of the technical confidence gained, to move more freely. Certainly his command of contrast, within numbers and across whole acts, is bolder and more assured, as is his judgement of how greater weight may be placed in the important dramatic passages without thereby trivialising the lighter dances and virtuoso diversions. He has developed greater freedom for himself in creating situations in which the 'lyrical idea' can find its best expression. No score of his possesses a finer flow of brilliant, attractive, memorable ideas; but it does so because of the strength and logic of the design. The sense of manufacture which Tchaikovsky deplored in his sonata structures is here absent, or rather is of the kind that came naturally to him; for what his structure here requires is a skilful sequence of ideas, well-contrasted and presented in attractive orchestration, to match the undemanding, unreal prettiness of the fairy story. Given a scenario as attractive as Vsevolozhsky's and a choreographic plot as intricate and efficient as Petipa's, he recognised that he was working with men of the highest professional skill; and he was resolved to match their standards with music of the kind for which he knew he had a special talent. He claimed to owe much to Delibes, and at the time of writing *The Sleeping Beauty* was studying Adam's *Giselle*; but as no other composer of his day, he was the master of music which, while delightful and satisfying in its own right, contains a sense of strong physical movement needing completion in dance.

PROLOGUE

Introduction

The music is based on two themes, the first that of the wicked fairy Carabosse:

Ex.12

and the second that of the good Lilac Fairy:

Ex.13

These are stated and to a limited extent developed in contrasting sections before the music moves into a march rhythm as a link to the first number.

No. 1: March

The guests are arriving at the palace of King Florestan XIV for the christening of Princess Aurora. They are shown to their places by the Master of Ceremonies, Catalabutte; the King and Queen enter.

The music is cast in the form of a rondo with two episodes. The march, at once lively and grandiose, is in A major, with the guests seen to be arriving as the curtain rises. Catalabutte has a so-called 'narration' as he arranges everyone in their places (first episode, in C sharp minor). After the return of the march, Catalabutte's second 'narration' is in F sharp minor; and during this the music rises to a climax, with horn fanfares, to announce the entry of the King and Queen. A decorated version of the march, richly scored for full orchestra, provides a suitably ceremonial close.

No. 2: Scène dansante

Fairies arrive with their pages and attendants to offer gifts to the baby Princess, last among them the Lilac Fairy. At a sign from Catalabutte, pages and young girls advance with their gifts.

The fairies enter to a gentle theme, very delicately scored, in the waltz rhythm which through the ballet tends to be associated with Aurora; after six bars in 4/4 as the pages come forward, another gentle waltz unites the guests.

No. 3: Pas de Six

The Fairies come forward with their gifts, arranging them around the cradle and accompanying them with the promise that the Princess shall grow up beautiful, talented, and kind.

A short Introduction (a) with sweeping harp arpeggios leads to the Adagio (b), actually marked Andante, in which the harp accompanies a graceful theme on the clarinet that is later, after another brief harp cadenza, transformed into an Allegro 2/4 version of the theme. There follows a set of six variations for the Fairies.

1. Candide. Petipa's original MS notes include a drawing of her, attended by two turbaned pages: she has been identified as representing a kind of phlox which in one version of the traditional

Language of Flowers stands for Beauty, but Petipa makes her carry a wand in the form of Canterbury Bells. The directness and simplicity of the music suggests that the intention was for her to symbolise the gift of candour. The movement is a short oboe solo against clarinet arpeggios over simple string chords.

2. Coulante: Fleur de farine. The reference is to a kind of convolvulus, in the Language of Flowers symbolising Grace. A lively 6/8 Allegro with prominent woodwind figuration.

3. Fée aux miettes. The 'crumbs' are those by Russian custom sprinkled on a cradle by the godmother to ensure that the child shall never go hungry. It is the most original of the variations. Over held low trombone chords, violins pick out a pizzicato quaver figure (presumably suggesting the crumbs), with a cello counter-figure presently added. The crumb figure passes to low strings, over jabbing chords on clarinet, bassoon and horn. The first section returns, with added flute and oboe trills. It lasts a mere forty-one bars of Allegro moderato, but the oddity of the textures, yet their haunting charm, make the movement a remarkable and apt feat of aural imagination in which themes play virtually no part.

4. Canari qui chante. The gift of eloquence. A racy little study conducted largely in piccolo and flute triplets, over pizzicato strings and miniature bells.

5. Violante. The gift of energy. After a vigorous opening, a lively dialogue between clarinet and strings in a single little semiquaver figure.

6. The Lilac Fairy. The gift of wisdom, which in Russian folklore a child will acquire if it is placed under lilacs. A graceful waltz.

Coda. An energetic Allegro giusto for all six fairies.

No. 4: Finale

As the Lilac Fairy approaches the cradle, a noise is heard without, and a page announces the wicked fairy Carabosse. She enters in a carriage drawn by rats, furious at not having been invited to be a godmother. Catalabutte is forced to admit his error, and when he casts himself at her feet she begins to tear out his hair, to the relish of her attendants. The good fairies beg her to be forgiving, but shrieking with laughter she gives Aurora her present – a curse. One day Aurora will prick her finger on a spindle and die. But the Lilac Fairy, who has not yet given her present to the princess, has her own magic powerful enough to counter some of this curse, and she turns death into a long sleep, from which Aurora will be woken after a hundred years by the kiss of a young Prince. The enraged Carabosse drives off in her carriage, while the good fairies and the King and Queen gather round the cradle.

This long finale, at once narrative and symphonic, both accompanies the rapidly moving sequence of events descriptively and brings up to the centre of the drama the conflict of good and evil as symbolised by the themes of the Lilac Fairy and Carabosse. The gentle opening is swiftly interrupted by agitated music leading to Carabosse's entry on a version of Ex. 12; and the tension of the music develops by alternation between this theme in various forms and passages representing the supplication of the King and Queen, Catalabutte's remorse, and the pleas for mercy from the good fairies. The approaches to Carabosse bring modified forms of her theme, until the last one leads into the theme of her curse:

Ex.14

After a passage describing the consternation of the Court, Carabosse leaves, to yet another version of her theme; and only as she vanishes does a rich, full development of the Lilac Fairy's theme intervene and bring the act to an end on a note of hope.

ACT 1: *The Spell*

No. 5: Scene

The Palace grounds are thronged with visitors come to celebrate Aurora's twentieth birthday. Among the villagers, Catalabutte notices some old women threading spindles – strictly forbidden since the day of Carabosse's curse. He removes the spindles, and orders the old women to be taken to prison. At that moment the King and Queen appear on the terrace, together with four foreign Princes, Charming, Avignon, Fleur-de-pois and Fortuné, who have come to seek her hand in marriage. Catalabutte is questioned about the disturbance, and is forced to reveal what has happened. The King threatens the women with death, but at the Princes' intercession pardons them.

The Act opens with another symphonic narration, in which the dominant factor is a version of the curse theme. However, the falling fourths are turned to fifths, and though the theme colours the invention, it is not brought to the fore as a kind of Fate motive except at the moment when Catalabutte spies the forbidden spindles. The music is vigorous, bright, cheerful; but the presence of the curse theme conveys an atmosphere of latent tension on the festivity. (Who could have foreseen that within a couple of decades the situation of a Royal child kept by its fearful parents from pricking its finger would become one of the issues that rocked the Tsar's throne?) The vigour of the music, rising to a climax on a diminished seventh to tonic cadence that embodies the falling fourths, is interrupted by the appearance of the Royal party to a theme of formal elegance. A new section develops out of the exchanges between the King and Catalabutte, once more rising to a climax and a pause. In a short final section, the four princes implore the King's mercy (a theme repeated fourfold and then tutti); and to this he consents in bassoon phrases that bring the movement to an end not on a positive full close but poised on a dominant seventh.

No. 6: Waltz

The rejoicings are resumed.

With the pardoning of the old women, the tension finds release in one of Tchaikovsky's best known and best loved waltzes, famous from innumerable performances but making its true effect as an expression of warmth and relaxation in the course of the drama. The scene is said to have been one of Petipa's best stagings.

No. 7: Scene

The four Princes approach the King and Queen as suitors for Aurora's hand. They have never seen her, and each in turn admires her portrait on a medallion. She enters and greets her parents.

The closeness with which Tchaikovsky followed Petipa's scenario in scenes of action has already been described in connection with this scene; and it serves to move the drama swiftly forward from this formal waltz to another of the score's most famous set pieces.

No. 8: Pas d'action

Aurora dances with the four Princes in turn, accepting from each the rose he offers her. The Maids of Honour, the Pages, and then Aurora herself again dance. She sees an old woman who proffers her a spindle wound with coloured thread. She accepts the gift, and begins to dance with it.

a) By way of a harp cadenza, the music moves into a 12/8 Adagio maestoso, the so-called Rose Adagio. It is a movement in Tchaikovsky's most impassioned style, portraying, as in the Fifth Symphony, love as an ideal and repeating between different episodes its fervent main tune scored in his richest vein.

b) As lively contrast, the maids of honour perform a sprightly dance whose theme is reworked and rescored for a dance by the pages.

c) Aurora's solo variation is to an elaborate violin solo moving from a steady Allegro moderato into an Allegro vivace.

d) Coda. Aurora begins her dance to a theme over a reiterated figure that is built up into a movement of great tension; and as she seizes the spindle, a waltz theme derived from the opening of her dance theme, but tense and somewhat distorted in manner, again begins to build up towards a climax.

No. 9: Finale

Aurora pricks her finger: she spins round faster and faster, and finally collapses on the ground. The old woman throws back her hood to reveal herself as Carabosse. The four Princes draw their swords, but she vanishes in a cloud of smoke. Then the Lilac Fairy appears and commands that Aurora be carried into the Palace. A mist rises; the courtiers grow still; flowers and undergrowth rise and cover the walls, until the Palace is lost to view in a vast forest.

Aurora pricks her finger to a fiercely scored derivation of Ex. 12.

Ex.15 **Allegro giusto**

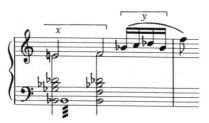

Out of prominent use in it of a version of the semiquaver figure
(*y*) her dance of giddiness develops.

Ex.16

Carabosse's poison is at work in her, and as she falls to the ground
the brass grind out an augmented version of the semiquaver
theme (*y*). A few bars of Andante reflect the horror of the court;
then, Allegro vivo, Carabosse's theme is stated plainly as she
reveals herself, and it is briefly developed before she vanishes. The
consternation and dismay of the Court are interrupted by the Lilac
Fairy: the key moves unexpectedly (by an enharmonic switch on
A flat = G sharp) from F minor to her own E major. Aurora is
borne away, and as the Lilac Fairy raises her wand, the figure of
Ex. 14, Carabosse's spell, is modified into a more benign aspect.

Ex.17

The ensuing transformation allows Tchaikovsky to indulge his
most subtle ear for scoring, as delicate, elaborate figuration gradually rises to dominate the repeated Lilac Fairy theme of Ex. 13; and
finally fragments of the theme die away behind tremolo strings and
harp. It is an ingenious and beautiful movement. The skilful use of
transformations of Carabosse's theme, as the crisis is reached, is not
only effectively worked so as to reflect the swift moving action,
but makes an effective contrast with the musical means of the
closing section. After Carabosse's dark, tortuous concealment and
conspiracy, expressed in the rapid transformations of her theme and

its overcoming of Aurora, the musical simplicity of the Lilac Fairy has a consoling directness; and the need to sustain this by variations of texture is ideally apt as a musical metaphor to the gradual growth around the Palace of the dense forest that both conceals and protects the Princess.

ACT 2

No. 10: Entr'acte and scene

A hunt is in progress, and presently hunters and huntresses enter to rest from the chase. They are followed by Prince Désiré and his tutor Gallifron, who proposes some diversions.

A hunting call motive on horns builds up to an exuberant climax, turning from 12/8 to an elegant 4/4 as the hunters arrive.

No. 11: Blind Man's Buff

During the game, the Prince stands aloof and uninterested in the girls' attentions.

A vigorous 4/4 Allegro vivo developing on full orchestra a tune given out by violas and cor anglais.

No. 12: Scene

a) Scene: Gallifron sets the dancers in their places.
b) Dance of the Duchesses.
c) Dance of the Baronesses.
d) Dance of the Countesses.
e) Dance of the Marchionesses.

The Duchesses have a minuet, the Baronesses a gavotte, the Countesses an energetic movement in 6/8 somewhat like a slow tarantella, the Marchionesses a nimbler 2/4 movement (they carry little arrows with which they goad their companions).

No. 13: Farandole

a) Scene.
The ladies propose a farandole in which the peasants accompanying the hunt may join.
b) Dance.

The Prince's beaters appear to be Poles rather than Provençals, for though a (6/8) farandole is proposed, they enjoy themselves to a lively mazurka.

Though it primarily serves the purpose of diversion, also giving an opportunity to smaller groups from the corps de ballet, this sequence of dances is well judged dramatically. The use of traditional dances helps to set the period, and by keeping them short, light, and formal, Tchaikovsky ensures that this courtly diversion is outside the main plot, merely emphasising its irrelevance to the melancholy, aloof Prince.

No. 14: Scene

As the hunt moves off again, the Prince remains behind, alone and pensive. Evening falls, and the Lilac Fairy appears in a mother-of-pearl boat drawn by two butterflies. She tells him the story of the Sleeping Beauty, and conjures up a vision of her. A second vision shows Aurora dancing with fairies in the forest. The Prince is prevented from catching her by the fairies.

The horns lead the hunt off over a long tonic pedal, and the Lilac Fairy appears, now in D flat and at first to a delicate, mysterious scoring of her theme (slightly altered) for piccolo, flute and cor anglais over tremolo strings. The music builds up to a rich climax with the narration: Aurora's dance is to a nimble 6/8 Allegro vivace.

No. 15: Pas d'action

Aurora dances with the Prince, then by herself; finally she vanishes.
a) Pas d'action. Aurora and Désiré meet, to a rich cello melody:
Ex.18

Andante cantabile

Cello *p molto espress.*

This has an obvious affinity with the second theme of the Fifth Symphony's slow movement, as it is taken over by strings:

Ex.19

Written in the year previously, the music of the Fifth Symphony's Andante cantabile is said to have been associated with a declaration of love on one of the drafts; and there can be little doubt that the symphony is here concerned with what Tchaikovsky once declared to be part of a symphony's role, to 'reveal those wordless urges that lie in the heart, asking earnestly for expression.' If the ballet's music is less fervent, it is because although the subject is again the release of love, the theme is not autobiographical but dramatic, less painfully immediate to Tchaikovsky himself. Aurora, with her capacity for love as revealed in the Rose Adagio, and Désiré, lonely and dissatisfied with his life, meet in the magic conjured up by the Lilac Fairy: it is a lyrical encounter that clearly touched Tchaikovsky deeply, and led him to turn to a similar vein of expression to that which he had once used for himself.

b) Aurora's Variation. Aurora is also, even within the spell holding forth a vision of ideal love, a lively young girl; and it is part of her character and her charm that her melody should be turned into a sprightly Allegro (over a dominant pedal: the use of tonic and dominant pedals is a technical characteristic of the whole work).

c) Coda. A nimbly scored Presto serves to return her to the world of the enchantment in which she still lies: it is a vision for Désiré, a dream for her, which the Lilac Fairy has contrived.

Petipa asked for 'a voluptuous Adagio; a short coquettish Allegro; Variation for Aurora and short coda. In the coda, music using mutes, 2/4, as in *A Midsummer Night's Dream*.' Tchaikovsky finishes with a very successful little Mendelssohnian scherzo, choosing not to mute his strings but writing with a deftness, delicacy and wit that exactly catch the spirit of Petipa's intentions.

No. 16: Scene

Overwhelmed by the vision of Aurora, Prince Désiré implores the Lilac Fairy to take him to her.

Though sometimes omitted, this brief scene has a point in establishing the Prince's ardour, after his previous melancholy, at the glimpse of love he has been shown.

No. 17: Panorama

The Lilac Fairy leads Prince Désiré in her boat through the enchanted wood to the Palace where Aurora lies sleeping.

One of the most famous features of the *ballet-pantomime, La Belle au bois dormant* by Scribe and Aumer, to Hérold's music, was the scene in which Prince Charming journeys to the castle of the Sleeping Beauty. Though Vsevolozhsky can never have seen this production, Petipa may well have done; and the device used for this scene remained a regular feature of the Paris Opéra. It consisted of a painted cloth mounted upon *manivelles*, revolving drums, so that the scenery unrolled across the stage while Prince Charming sat in a gently rocking boat. The illusion of a journey thereby created impressed many composers, including none other than Wagner (who used it in modified form, together with other devices taken from Cicéri's productions at the Opéra, as late as *Parsifal*). Petipa's note, 'Continuous music depending on the length of the panorama', must indicate that a similar device was intended. The serene, gliding melody over throbbing chords is in turn clearly designed to act as a background to a transformation of some kind.

No. 18: Entr'acte

Tchaikovsky did not envisage the *Panorama* as completing the change of scene, as is shown by his composition of this beautiful entr'acte, a meditation for solo violin (Ex. 20). That love is again the subject of the piece is suggested by the affinity of its main theme with Hermann's declaration of love in *The Queen of Spades*.

The Entra'acte was intended for Leopold Auer to perform, but was discarded even before the première as prolonging the action excessively: this practice has usually been followed by Western producers, though Frederick Ashton reinserted it after No. 19 as an 'Awakening Pas de Deux' for Aurora and Désiré for his 1968 Royal Ballet production.

Ex.20

(a) The Sleeping Beauty

Andante sostenuto

mf con passione

(b) The Queen of Spades

Andante

p

Scene 2

No. 19: Symphonic Entr'acte (The Sleep) and Scene

Clouds enveloping the scene gradually disperse to reveal the Lilac Fairy leading Prince Désiré through the tangled undergrowth to the Palace. He gazes at the Sleeping Beauty; then, recognising her as the Princess of his vision, he kisses her.

Under a high muted tremolo violin note, woodwind softly give out a version of the chords at (*x*) in Ex. 15, answered by a rapid *pp* statement of Ex. 12. Through this very delicately scored music of Carabosse's enchantment there sounds the Lilac Fairy's theme (Ex. 13) on muted trumpet. A new melodic figure is heard, first on cor anglais and then on oboe; but it is almost more part of the texture than a theme. The clouds clear, to a repetition of the woodwind chords, and with the appearance of the Lilac Fairy and Prince Désiré the music changes to a vigorous Allegro. The chromatic figure of Ex. 15 (*x*) continues to sound through the texture as the Prince approaches her, to turn into plain descending arpeggios as he stoops over her and kisses her. Though essentially music to accompany a stage picture, the scene is skilfully composed to reinforce the mysterious atmosphere of the enchanted forest with the musical imagery of delicate, entwined melodic lines and hazy textures, but also with a very carefully worked use of Carabosse's theme as the force that holds the enchantment together and is finally overcome.

No. 20: Finale

Aurora awakens, and seeing the Prince of whom she has dreamt, she takes him in her arms. Light floods the Palace; the courtiers and servants slowly stir to life; the weeds that have grown over the room die back, and the cobwebs fall. The spell is broken.

The music is strong and direct, with a suggestion of Court formality in a slower middle section; and the curtain falls to the rising chromatic figure on brass now sounding out triumphantly.

ACT 3

No. 21: March

In the Great Hall of the Palace, the courtiers greet the King and Queen, who are led in by Catalabutte together with the betrothed couple, Princess Aurora and Prince Désiré, for the wedding celebrations.

A formal march, bright and ceremonial, with a trio section.

No. 22: Polacca

Ceremonial entry of a number of Perrault's fairy-tale characters.

A brilliant dance to introduce the succeeding characteristic dances. Petipa's original plan for this to begin with four quadrilles, Turkish, Ethiopian, African and American, was dropped.

No. 23: Pas de quatre

Introduction: Variation I – The Golden Fairy; Variation II – The Silver Fairy; Variation III – The Sapphire Fairy; Variation IV – The Diamond Fairy; Coda.

The Introduction, a graceful 6/8 movement, brings the four fairies forward. The Golden Fairy has a somewhat heavy-footed waltz. The Silver Fairy tinkles agreeably with the lightest of scoring that includes a glockenspiel. Petipa marked the Sapphire Fairy, 'Pentahedral. Music in five beats', with a piece of quaint literal-mindedness (misplaced, moreover, since a sapphire in fact crystal-lises in the hexagonal system). However, Tchaikovsky was ob-viously taken with the idea, and responded with a lively Viva-cissimo in 5/4. It was a rhythm he used again in the famous limping waltz of the *Pathetic Symphony*, but also, less familiarly, in the *Valse à cinqtemps*, No. 16 of his Eighteen Piano Pieces, Op. 72, of 1893.

For the Diamond Fairy, Petipa requested, 'brilliant, shining, like electricity, fast 2/4' – a fair description of what Tchaikovsky gave him. The energetic Coda serves to bring all four dancers together again and to dismiss them.

No. 24: Pas de caractère: Puss in Boots and the White Cat

The two cats dance to music which most ingeniously imitates their mewing, purring, yowling and occasional spitting.

No. 25: Pas de quatre

Cinderella, Prince Fortuné, the Blue Bird and Princess Florine.
   A flute solo, joined by clarinet in imitation, over a light string accompaniment, introduces the four dancers. Variation I is a powerful waltz for Cinderella and Prince Fortuné, Variation II a delicate Andantino, with flute twitterings, for the Blue Bird and Princess Florine. Once again a Coda gathers together the dancers. The number was choreographed by Petipa from the outset as a pas de deux, which is why he asked for the later No. 26b to provide a dance for Cinderella and Prince Fortuné.

No. 26: Pas de caractère

a) Red Riding Hood and the Wolf.
   Tripping figuration, pursued by fearsome growls in the strings, ending in a più mosso.
b) Cinderella and Prince Fortuné.
   An Allegro agitato that moves into a waltz which increases in speed to a last-minute Presto. Written later at Petipa's request, and intended to accompany a dance showing the Prince discovering Cinderella by means of the glass slipper.

No 27: Pas Berrichon

Hop-o'-my-thumb, his brothers and the Ogre.
   Another short descriptive piece, with lively figuration for Hop-o'-my-thumb and an awkward, lumbering theme for the Ogre.

No. 28: Pas de deux

Aurora and Désiré.
Introduction (four bars of Allegretto).

a) Entrance. A lyrical Allegro moderato, with a warm, 6/8 melody on strings and woodwind.

b) Adagio. The 6/8 movement, perhaps associated with the characteristic 'good' rhythm of the Lilac Fairy, is continued, Andante non troppo, with a tender theme first given out by the oboe over pizzicato strings. There is a similar resemblance to the Lilac Fairy's flowing theme.

Var. 1. Désiré. A Vivace 6/8 moving into a 2/4 Prestissimo, inviting virtuoso display from the dancer but essentially an expression of exuberance and energy.

Var. 2. Aurora. An Andantino which brings back the solo violin. At once elegant and sprightly, it serves to remind the listener that, although a hundred years have passed, Aurora is still a girl of twenty.

Coda. Intended to bring the lovers together in a dance of vigorous happiness.

This pas de deux is the 'love duet' of the ballet, the first occasion on which their tenderness for each other is expressed in a full lyrical movement that also gives expression to their individual characters. It is perhaps placed surprisingly late for a love duet; but it makes its effect in the structure. We do not meet Aurora at all in the Prologue, when she is in her cradle; Act 1 is hers; Act 2 is Désiré's: here at last the two meet properly, and it is obviously right to place this substantial pas de deux after the delightful but incidental divertissement. The music shows us a happy ending achieved, the love duet coming as they are joined in marriage. As in other works of art, this reservation until the dénouement of the full statement of love, between two people who have had to undergo complicated trials and difficulties, is exceptionally moving in effect. Perhaps Tchaikovsky had in mind a book he particularly admired, *Little Dorrit,* with its glowing resolution at the end of much distress, complexity and disarray. Even in the lighter context of a fairy ballet, which tells a simple magical story for an audience that demanded much in the way of diversion, the device can in the hands of major artists make a potent effect; and so it does here. The movement is beautifully planned, moving from expressions of mutual rapture through moments of individual delight to the final vigorous, optimistic dance together. The coda belongs by right to the lovers: the tradition, common since Diaghilev's 1921 production, of handing it over to 'The Three Ivans' for a squatting *prisyadka* is presumably based on the very Russian vigour that informs the music.

No. 29: Sarabande

No indication is given of the dancers for this little-heard number; but we may suppose that it was intended for the full company, dancing a formal sarabande in the style of Louis XIV's Versailles, Petipa's avowed model for the staging of this Act at the Court of 'Florestan XIV'.

No. 30: Finale

The guests and those who have taken part in the entertainment parade around the floor.

A vigorous mazurka, scored for full orchestra, with two shorter contrasting episodes.

No. 31: Apotheosis

The Lilac Fairy appears, to bless the marriage, in a final tableau.

Moving back two generations to Louis XIV's grandfather Henry of Navarre, *le grand Béarnais* of pious gastronomic memory, Tchaikovsky bases his final number on the old French tune 'Vive Henri IV': this he knew from the collection *Chants et chansons de France* discussed on pp. 69–70.

Ex.21

Vive Hen-ri Quat-re, vi-ve ce roi vail-lant

Ce dia-ble à quat-re a le tri-ple tal-ent, de boire et de

batt-re et d'être un vert gal-ant

The tune was very popular throughout the nineteenth century: Dussek had put it into general currency with a set of variations, and it occurs frequently in Bishop's 'musical romance' *Henri Quatre, or Paris in the Olden Times* (1820). Tchaikovsky was fond of it, and was to use a version of it in Scene 4 of *The Queen of Spades*. Here, in the ballet, it was proposed by Petipa (or at any rate appears in his synopsis) following the suggestion in Perrault: the Prince, on awakening the Princess in the supposed time of Louis XIV, finds that she is naturally still wearing the high collar and other clothes of a hundred years before.

The Nutcracker

In Vsevolozhsky's eyes, if not those of all his public, *The Sleeping Beauty* was a success, and was given on twenty-one of the forty-five ballet evenings in the second, 1890–1, season. It was therefore not long before he was casting about for another way of employing Tchaikovsky's gifts in the theatre. Tchaikovsky was also interested in renewing the collaboration, and the idea developed of a double bill consisting of an opera and a ballet. He wrote to Modest from Kamenka at the beginning of January 1891 with a suggestion for an opera: 'Give a thought to *King René's Daughter*. I shall probably go to Italy to compose, and I need a subject by the end of January. And what ballet?' The answer to his question in fact lay in his own library, for on 3 February 1882 he had written from Rome to thank Sergey Flerov, a critic and journalist of his acquaintance, for a copy of E. T. A. Hoffmann's story *Nussknacker und Mausekönig* (1816) in Flerov's new Russian translation. Perhaps he also remembered that his beloved *Coppélia* was based on a Hoffmann story, *Der Sandmann*. Before long plans were settling on a one-act opera on Henrik Hertz's story *King René's Daughter* (eventually entitled, after its heroine, *Yolanta*) and a two-act ballet after Hoffmann's story, *The Nutcracker*.

Though ostensibly a children's fairy tale, Hoffmann's original is a strange piece of work mingling reality and fantasy on several levels. It is set on Christmas Eve in the house of Medizinilrat Stahlbaum. There arrives the peculiar figure of 'Uncle' Drosselmeier: Hoffmann had had considerable childhood experience of eccentric uncles, and had himself become one to the family of his publisher friend Hitzig. He makes Drosselmeier bring a model castle just such as he had himself once constructed as a stage design for Burg Ringstetten in his opera *Undine*; and he also presents the children, Fritz and Marie, with the curious Nutcracker, for which Marie conceives tender feelings that it seems in some way to return. Drosselmeier, we are told, is 'in no way a handsome man, but small and emaciated, with a very wrinkled face and instead of a right eye a huge black patch'. Hoffmann, who was obsessed with his own ugliness, is clearly caricaturing himself. That night, a battle takes place between the Mouse King (who has seven heads) and the children's toys, especially Fritz's soldiers under the generalship of the Nutcracker: Hoffmann describes their battle order with a military efficiency that won the compliments of the Prussian general Gneisenau, who particularly commended the strategic value of placing a battery on the commanding position of Mama's footstool. Only the intervention of Marie, throwing her slipper, settles the outcome. Next morning, Marie refuses to believe that these happenings were a dream; and Drosselmeier returns to see the children, telling them a story of Princess Pirlipat and the Mouse Queen into which is woven events from the domestic life of the Stahlbaums and from Marie's 'dream'. Princess Pirlipat is protected from the avenging Mouse Queen, and her father welcomes visiting kings and princes with a sausage-feast. There are further fantastic complications with the enchantment of the princess, who can only be restored to her beauty by a young man who can with his own teeth crack the great nut Krakatuk. The story is told at a meeting of the Serapionsbrüder, the mythical gathering which Hoffmann, anticipating Schumann, peopled with characters who are aspects of his own personality. The author of *Nussknacker* is Lothar, who in general represents Hoffmann's somewhat sardonic, sceptical side.

Rather than a mere fairy story, then, this is a *Novelle* (it runs to fifty closely printed pages in Georg Ellinger's standard edition of 1912), and one which involves a complicated layering of fantasy and reality in Hoffmann's characteristic vein. This extends from the fictional framing of the story, as told by one part of Hoffmann while he simultaneously appears in it as Drosselmeier (who is also one of the figures in the model castle and who frightens Marie by transforming himself into the owl clock), to the uncertainty as to whether Marie has really dreamt the battle and how Drosselmeier knows about it, and then to the tale-within-a-tale of Princess Pirlipat and the Nutcracker. In another way, there is an uncertainty as to whether the story is really meant for children or not. Theodor, another of the Serapionsbrüder, is made to point out that the threads are difficult to follow; there are some lofty philosophical asides; and the Nutcracker first addresses his troops in tones reminiscent of Frederick the Great ('Kein Hund von Trompeter regt und rührt sich!'), then at the height of the battle exclaiming, in an allusion few German children would have got in 1816, 'A horse! a horse! my kingdom for a horse!' Hoffmann, in short, is pretending to write a children's story; but he is characteristically using it as a mask for something more peculiar.

Almost all of this is watered down to make it acceptable to the conventions of *ballet-féerie* as Petipa saw them. The first part of the plot survives more or less intact in outline, if not so much in atmosphere, and various allusions give clues to the ballet treatment, such as mention of pine forests and an emphasis on eating, particularly on confectionery; but the disturbing eccentricity which is the essence of the tale survives only in the figure of Drosselmeier. For the rest, the battle is taken as an excuse for an amusing stage diversion, while the lame second part of the ballet is no more than another excuse for divertissements of another sort. Hoffmann's Marie is rendered by her adventures a dreamy, introspective child, roused from her reveries by the Nutcracker now become Drosselmeier's nephew: he bears her off to be his bride in Marzipanschloss. Clara, in the ballet, is merely taken off into the Kingdom of Sweets, where after the pretty dances everyone does her honour for saving the Prince.

To begin with, it was the opera that absorbed most of Tchaikovsky's attention. He was doubtful about the subject of the ballet; he was beginning to feel older, less fluent; worst, he was smarting under the recent decision by Nadezhda von Meck to break off their relationship. This meant some financial hardship, but the real blow was rejection by a woman who was to some extent a surrogate mother to him. He set to work on planning the ballet, working on it 'with all my might', he told Modest on 9 March, so as to get it out of the way before he left on a tour of America. He conferred with Petipa about it in St Petersburg on 18 March, also holding discussions with the Directors of the Imperial Theatres. So keen was he to get the ballet finished, he told his brother Anatoly, that he continued working on it during his journey to Berlin and on to Paris, lamenting in Le Havre, as he awaited his ship, 'the absolute impossibility of depicting the Sugar-Plum Fairy in music'. To Taneyev he had complained, 'I began the ballet with an effort, sensing a decline in my inventive powers'; Bob Davydov was told that it was 'far weaker than *The Sleeping Beauty*'. 'If I become convinced that I can only set *rechauffés* at my musical banquet,' he continued, 'then I shall certainly give up composing', and he added in the same letter a grisly account of his hair turning white and, like his teeth, falling out, his feet dragging, his eyes dimming and all his other faculties failing. Whatever the drama in this account by a life-long hypochondriac, it was true that he had aged: he had begun to tire more easily, and his friends thought him older than his fifty years. When he concentrated on the opera, determined to produce the best of which he was capable, he found his thoughts straying to the ballet; yet the ballet seemed less important than the opera.

One good card he did feel he had up his sleeve. As early as February 1891 he had decided on the use of children's instruments, having been captivated by their effect in Haydn's *Toy Symphony* and Bernhard Romberg's *Kinder-Symphonie*. He bought some in Paris, and those eventually used in the score of *The Nutcracker* were trumpet, drum, rattle, cuckoo, quail, cymbals, and two so-called *tamburi conigli* or rabbit drums, miniature drums for playing by characters on stage. Better still, he had come upon a new instrument. To Pyotr Jürgenson he wrote, on 15 June 1891,

I have discovered a new orchestral instrument in Paris, something between a small piano and a Glockenspiel, with a divinely beautiful tone. I want to introduce this instrument into the symphonic poem *The Voyevoda* and the ballet. The instrument is called the Celesta Mustel and costs 1200fr. You can only buy it from the inventor, Mustel, in Paris. I want to ask you to order one of these instruments. . . . Have it sent direct to Petersburg; but no-one there must know about it. I am afraid that Rimsky-Korsakov and Glazunov might hear of it and make use of the new effect before I can. I expect a colossal effect from this new instrument.

So completely is the effect associated with the Sugar-Plum Fairy's dance that it is surprising to find a note in Tchaikovsky's score accepting that in the absence of the celesta the part might be played on the piano.

Work on the ballet continued throughout 1891, though a further interruption came with a tour at the end of the year that took him to Warsaw and then on to Hamburg. Here some problems over the translation of recitative passages led him to hand the performance of *Eugene Onegin* over to the local conductor who was, he told Bob Davydov on 19 January, 'not some mediocrity but a man of *genius* who is longing to conduct the first performance'. It was Gustav Mahler; and the performance justified all Tchaikovsky's hopes. But beset with homesickness, he cancelled part of the tour and returned home to Maidanovo, where he scored part of the now completed ballet to make a concert suite which he could conduct to replace a performance of his tone-poem *The Voyevoda* at a St Petersburg concert on 19 March. It was announced, with French titles, in the form and order that has remained traditional: I. Ouverture miniature. II. Danses caractéristiques: a) Marche b) Danse de la Fée-Dragée c) Trépac, danse russe d) Danse arabe e) Danse chinoise f) Danse des mirlitons. III. Valse des fleurs. The success of this first hearing of the *Nutcracker* music was so great that most of the numbers were encored. The Moscow première of the Suite followed on 16 July under Vojtěch Hlaváč, at the first concert at the Electric Exhibition. The complete ballet had been finally orchestrated at Maidanovo on 4 April.

After the success of their collaboration over *The Sleeping Beauty*, it was natural that Tchaikovsky and Petipa should work in a similar manner for the new ballet. Accordingly, Petipa, who had read the translation by Alexandre Dumas *père* (1845, republished 1881), provided another scenario; this was again drafted in French, and in it he set out in the same meticulous detail his notes of the intended action and dance plan, together with suggestions for the music, leaving large margins for additions. However, during the winter Petipa, now in his seventies, fell ill and was unable to begin work on the production. Accordingly the task passed into the hands of Lev Ivanov, who had gained experience in working with Petipa on *The Sleeping Beauty* as well as being himself an artist of great distinction and versatility. He had devised the dances for Borodin's *Prince Igor* and Rimsky-Korsakov's *Mlada*; he was also a gifted amateur musician, who once astonished Anton Rubinstein (a man not easily overawed by the musical feats of others) by playing through from memory, almost complete after one hearing, Rubinstein's opera *The Vine*. Even allowing for exaggeration, the feat was clearly remarkable, the more so since Ivanov was unable to write down even the music he composed himself. There is further evidence that he was able to play whole ballets from memory; and he was quick to respond to the larger symphonic implications in Tchaikovsky's score. He had been responsible for two lakeside scenes (Acts 2 and 4) in *Swan Lake*, and indeed Act 2 has survived with his choreography virtually intact because it is so musical a conception. He is said to have been somewhat constrained by the number of short dances in the divertissements, though he composed for himself a Jester's Dance, with a hoop, which he performed at the première of the ballet on 18 December 1892.

The cast of the first performance consisted of Felix Kshesinsky (President Silberhaus), Augusta Ogoleit (Frau Silberhaus), Stanislava Belinskaya (Clara), Vasily Stukolkin (the Prince), Lydia Rubstova (Marianna), Timofey Stukolkin (Drosselmeier), Maria and Elizaveta Onegina (the President's relations), Sergey Legat (the Nutcracker), Nikolay Lozhkin (the President's servant), Antonietta dell'Era (the Sugar-Plum Fairy), Pavel Gerdt (Prince Coqueluche), and Ivanov as the Majordomo; Riccardo Drigo conducted, taking over from Eduard Nápravník, who had conducted *Yolanta*. 'The staging of both was splendid,' Tchaikovsky wrote to his brother Anatoly, 'but that of the ballet even too splendid – one's eyes grew tired of this luxuriance.' The *St Petersburg Gazette* was unenthusiastic about the music: 'A more tedious work was never seen ... the music is a long way from what is necessary for a ballet.' It was the old complaint of those entrenched in the habits which Tchaikovsky was going some way to overthrow. But he was winning over critics and listeners. The *St Petersburg News-sheet* wrote, on 19 December (o.s.),

Concerning the music of this ballet, it is hard to say which number is best, for everything from beginning to end is beautiful, melodious, original and individual.

And Mikhail Ivanov, in *The New Age* on 26 December (o.s.), preferred *The Nutcracker* to *Yolanta*:

The composer's technical mastery is expressed in this score in a brilliant manner at every step, and to enumerate the pages where Mr. Tchaikovsky shows himself a fine symphonist and a master of the orchestra would take too long: such pages are too numerous.

It is the praise for the melodiousness of the individual numbers and for the orchestral mastery which is the more accurate. Though there are substantial passages of quasi-symphonic development called for by the plot, especially in Act 1, these are not among the most characteristic or most effective that Tchaikovsky had written; and the essential nature of the ballet is contained in the separate numbers (as Tchaikovsky perhaps recognised when he allowed some of the best of them to act as a 'trailer' to the work in concert performance). The plot of *The Nutcracker* offers no opportunity for further development along the lines opened up by *Swan Lake* and *The Sleeping Beauty*. But it did allow Tchaikovsky to indulge to the full his taste for *le joli*. Reducing his gift for the 'lyrical idea' to the scope of the ballet and its many characteristic dances, he achieved the greatest refinement yet of his idiom in this vein; and the outcome is an entertainment of genius. Out of the association of a particular tone colour and its ideal melody, including the novel sound of the celesta, he devises moments of exquisite charm, limited in expressive range but enduringly memorable. It is by intention chocolate-box music, the music of Confiturenburg, the Kingdom of Sweets; and its success is to be measured by the deliciousness of its varied effects – the pretty chords of the three flutes for the *mirlitons,* the nimble flute of the Chinese Dance, the tripping strings of the miniature overture, the lightly dancing rhythms and scoring of the march (one of nursery harmlessness), above all Tchaikovsky's treasured effect, the succulent combination of the ethereal celesta with the soft murmur of the bass clarinet. Such orchestration is not merely a presentation of the melodies but an expressive aspect of them. For all his depression and his worry over his inventive powers, Tchaikovsky seems to have taken some pride and pleasure in his mastery of this art of escape; if it was no more than an unreal daydream of a good child rewarded with sweets, Tchaikovsky none the less found in it a certain poignancy as well as charm, as he looked back to the rosy vision of his own nursery days.

Overture

The 'miniature' atmosphere is immediately set, characteristically, by the scoring, which is for woodwind (with only an occasionally discreet reinforcement on horns) and a string ensemble consisting of divided first violins, divided second violins, and divided violas. There is thus no bass weight, but ample occasion for nimble counterpoint and for subtly detailed scoring to sustain the delicate tune.

ACT I

Scene 1

No. 1: Scene

It is Christmas Eve in the home of President Silberhaus of the Town Council and his children, Clara and Fritz. The parents are decorating the Christmas tree. Nine o'clock strikes on a clock consisting of an owl which flaps its wings at each stroke. The children burst into the room with some friends.

A graceful violin theme, over a pedal D and a rising scale counterpoint, accompanies the decoration of the tree. There is a more whimsical central section, with scherzando banter between clarinet, bassoon and flute. On its return, the opening section is interrupted by a weird passage for the owl clock: it is one of the few passages in the score where some of the atmosphere of Hoffmann's original survives. But the disturbing note of strangeness is brushed aside by the entry of the children to a cheerful 6/8 Allegro vivace on chattering woodwind. A harp cadenza accompanies the President's order for a march to be played.

No. 2: March

All join in a lively march round the room.

In Petipa's original programme, the children were to receive paper costumes and then to perform a series of masquerade dances – Chinese, Spanish, Italian (a tarantella), English (a jig), Russian (a trepak), French (based on the Carmagnole) and then a general dance, 'a frenzied galop'. During the planning of the ballet this was dropped and does not even survive into Petipa's MS scenario as submitted to Tchaikovsky; but some of the partly sketched masquerade suite became the Act 2 divertissement (the English dance was dropped altogether, to survive only as an outline printed as an appendix to the score: it was orchestrated by Leonard Salzedo for inclusion in a revised production by London Festival Ballet during the 1960s, when it was added to the Act 2 divertissement, and retained in Ronald Hynd's 1976 production for the same company, as a solo for Fritz in Act 1). The march which, much more economically, is all that remains is neatly constructed: the miniature fanfare on clarinets and brass is answered by a skipping dotted-note figure on strings with a scalic counterpoint, and ingenious variations of this make the first section. The tiny middle section, consisting of pattering semiquavers on flutes and violins, quickly reintroduces the opening music, which is then developed by Glinka-style variation with constantly changed accompaniment figures and orchestration.

No. 3: Children's galop and entrance of the parents

Everyone joins in a galop; then the other children's parents enter, in the clothes of merveilleuses *and* incroyables (*the slang for fops and dandies at the time of the Revolution and Directory*). *A general dance follows.*

A three-part dance. The first section is a light galop for the children, again using Tchaikovsky's favourite device of scale counterpoints. The Andante for the entrance of the *merveilleuses* and *incroyables* is to a formal minuet, a pastiche of French classical style. The third section introduces a popular tune, Allegro, 'Bon voyage, cher Dumollet'. This is mentioned in Petipa's scenario, though the idea may have come from Tchaikovsky himself. The version he uses (Ex. 22) is identical with that given (in D major) in Charles Lebouc's *Récréations de l'Enfance* (?1885); a slightly different version, to slightly different words, appears in a volume he had in his library (see below, p. 69).

No. 4: Scene

At the last stroke of the clock, there enters Councillor Drosselmeier, Clara's godfather. The children are alarmed at his odd appearance, until they see that he has brought them toys – a mechanical doll, toy soldiers, Harlequin, Columbine, etc. These he produces from a large cabbage and a large pie, to the children's delight.

Petipa requested for Drosselmeier music that was 'serious, somewhat frightening, then comic'; and Tchaikovsky's theme for him brilliantly catches the Hoffmannesque grimaces, the sinister-comic aspect of the old man (Ex. 23).

The atmosphere lightens as (Allegro vivace) the toys emerge from the cabbage and the pie, and a general waltz (not one of Tchaikovsky's best) then follows. Finally, a Presto 2/4 confirms the atmosphere of gaiety.

Ex.22

Bon voy - a - ge, cher Du-mol-let, { 1. à St. Ma - lo dé-barquez sans nau-
{ 2. et fix-ez vous dans ce

Fine

fra - ge!   1. Là vous ver - rez les deux mains dans les
lieu s'il vous plaît. 2. Des gens biens faits, des tor-tus, des ban-

poch - es, All - ez ven - ir des sag - es et des fous
croch - es

D.C. al Fine

Nul ne ser - a jamb - é si bien que vous.

Ex.23

Andantino

Viola
f

f *ff*   *marcatissimo*

No. 5: Scene and Grossvater Dance

Clara and Fritz want to take the toys away, but when they are not allowed to, Clara bursts into tears and Fritz throws a tantrum. Drosselmeier consoles them with a third toy – a huge nutcracker, in the shape of a man, which enchants Clara. Fritz hears the noise of the nuts cracking, and tries to seize the nutcracker; when she reluctantly lets him play with it, he tries to crack a nut so big that it is the nutcracker which breaks. Clara picks up the broken nutcracker and cradles it in her arms; she then takes her favourite doll out of its cot and puts the nutcracker there instead, singing a lullaby over it while the boys play around her. The scene ends with a general Grossvater dance.

A waltz passage (in 6/8) accompanies Drosselmeier's gift of the nutcracker, which is set to work to an elegant 2/4 tune that includes the rattle to represent its cracking of the nuts. This theme is distorted and speeded up with Fritz's intervention until the nutcracker breaks, *fff*. To a gentle derivative of part of the nutcracker theme, Clara nurses the broken toy. Petipa had requested a 'polka-berceuse': Tchaikovsky provides one, gently scored for flutes with woodwind accompaniment, in 2/4. It is twice interrupted by the vigorous theme of the boys, playing their toy trumpets and drums and other instruments. The finale of the scene is again a general dance, the traditional *Grossvatertanz* – also known as the *Kehraus* because it was the signal for everyone to leave. Tchaikovsky's version (not quite the same as that made familiar by Schumann and other composers, who included Spohr) retains the traditional contrast between a heavy 3/8 and a fast 2/4, the latter repeated at increasing speed. His version was taken from a folksong collection in his library, *Danses favorites et modernes*, where it appears as No. 21.

Ex.24

No. 6: Scene

The guests take their leave, and the children are sent to bed. Clara is not allowed to take the broken nutcracker with her, and goes with reluctance having tucked it up well. Night falls, and the moon lights up the empty room. Clara steals back to see her nutcracker, which seems to be giving off a mysterious light. Midnight strikes: the owl clock assumes the aspect of Drosselmeier, adding to Clara's fears. She tries to run away, but her legs will not carry her. Mice appear on all sides, and she collapses on a chair: they disappear. The Christmas tree grows enormously in size.

A graceful swaying theme for the departing guests is taken over by the cor anglais in an elaborated form as Clara is sent to bed. Tchaikovsky now paints a sinister nocturne with the aid of various conventional figures imaginatively deployed – tremolo strings, harp glissandos, flute skirls and a staccato figure on two piccolos over a very low *ppp* tuba and so on, until a distorted version of Ex. 23 on clarinet over ticking bassoons indicates the Drosselmeier-clock. By gradual development and intensification of a theme curiously reminiscent of Ex. 20 from *The Sleeping Beauty*, growing to a rich statement on full orchestra, the change of atmosphere to one of magic, with the mysterious growing of the Christmas tree, is suggested.

No. 7: Scene

The sentinel challenges, and getting no answer fires a shot; he arouses the drummer rabbits, who sound the alarm. The soldiers and the mice range themselves in battle order. The mice win the battle, and devour the ginger-bread soldiers. The Nutcracker summons his Old Guard, and the King of the Mice is welcomed by his troops. In the second battle, Clara throws her slipper at the Mouse King, and kills him. The Nutcracker becomes a handsome Prince, and offers Clara a journey to his kingdom.

The opening passages mimic ingeniously the toy sentinel and his alarm, and the gathering of the toy forces, by use of traditional military sounds (rataplan rhythms, arpeggio trumpet calls) scored with a lightness that keeps any suggestion of a real battle at a distance. Nevertheless, the vigour with which it is handled skil-fully generates a real tension, in the midst of which Clara's sudden action comes as a shock which halts the music and turns it towards a slow, curving figure on strings leading into the next scene.

Scene 2

No. 8: Scene

The room is transformed into a pine forest, with gnomes gathered round the Christmas tree with torches, doing honour to Clara, the Prince and the victorious toys. Snow is falling, and the gnomes guide Clara and the Prince on their way.

Over arpeggios on two harps, a broad tune is built up with rich orchestration: nothing so expansive or openly emotional has yet occurred in the score, indicating that a new condition has come over the story with the revealing of the Nutcracker as a Prince and the translation of Clara into his magic realm beyond the confines of her house, and of her childhood.

No. 9: Waltz of the Snowflakes

They are met by the King and Queen, who join their subjects in a swirling waltz.

The music is clearly designed to accompany a stage picture, and a photograph of the first production shows the corps de ballet with haloes of cotton-wool snowflakes against a backcloth of the winter forest. The music, which is at first based on a fluttering little flute figure across the waltz rhythm, does not constitute one of Tchaikovsky's most successful waltzes, though it must be said that its purpose is panoramic and illustrative rather than purely for dancing; and the loyal Laroche found in it, 'a feeling of shivering from the cold and the play of snowflakes in the moonlight'. At a change to 2/4, a wordless children's choir intones a figure in thirds, which is also taken up by flutes as the tempo eases for the final section.

ACT 2

Scene 3

No. 10: Scene

In the palace of the Kingdom of Sweets, Confiturenburg, the Sugar-Plum Fairy appears to welcome the travellers to the delights of her kingdom.

A gently lulling, amorous 6/8 theme raises the curtain on the palace, with swirling flute, piccolo and clarinet scales and throbbing horns emphasising the richness of the scene. The Sugar-Plum

Fairy appears with rippling celesta scales and harp arpeggios accompanying the main theme on violin harmonics: it is a sound of the delicate sweetness that exactly suits the subject, and must indeed have surprised and entranced the first audience.

No. 11: Scene

Beside a river of rose-water, Clara and the Prince appear and are welcomed to the Great Hall of the palace. The Prince is greeted by his sister, and tells how Clara saved his life. She is thanked profusely, and the company settle down to a splendid banquet and a divertissement.

Rich and delicate scoring surrounds the arrival of the travellers, with the Sugar-Plum Fairy's celesta and harp prominent together with flutter-tongued flutes and sensuous clarinet and bassoon flourishes. A livelier passage for the pages leading Clara and the Prince forward introduces the scene in which, Allegro agitato, the Prince recounts how Clara saved his life: this is to a rapid symphonic assembly of themes from the battle in Act 1; and a warm, stately theme leads to the setting of the banquet and (with some rising chromatic scales of expectation) the preparation of the divertissement.

No. 12: Divertissement

It was in the divertissement that Tchaikovsky's collaboration with Petipa was at its closest, in that he followed with remarkable precision the instructions given him. As in *The Sleeping Beauty*, he seems to have found the discipline stimulating, especially at a time when he feared that his own inventive powers were running at a low ebb; and when he did deviate substantially from what was demanded of him, it was to a purpose. It is worth comparing Petipa's scenario with the music throughout this celebrated divertissement:

a) Chocolate (Spanish Dance). Petipa: 'Spanish dance, 3/4, for 64 to 80 bars.' Allegro brillante, 3/4, seventy-eight bars: a vigorous dance with an athletic trumpet solo and the inescapable castanets.
b) Coffee (Arabian dance). Petipa: 'Arabia, Kingdom of Yemen (?). Café mocca. Oriental dance. 24–32 bars, sweet and charming music.' Commodo, 3/8, 102 bars. Tchaikovsky's much longer dance arises from his ingenious use of a lullaby from Georgia, 'Iav, nana' ('Sleep; lullaby'), which he took from Ippolitov-

Ivanov's collection according to the latter's memoirs, *Fifty Years of Russian Music*. The original, according to the ethnomuscicologist Dmitry Arakishvili, ran as follows:

Ex.25

Tchaikovsky's version is as follows:

Ex.26

Virtually all he has done is to add a drone ostinato bass, ingeniously varied in the middle section, with a few discreet touches of colour such as the tingle of a tambourine; yet the artistry is such that the tune seems ideally presented. The metronome marking is surprisingly fast: the piece is normally played a good deal slower.

c) Tea (Chinese dance). Petipa: '3/4 Allegretto Chinese type dance, little bells etc. 48 bars.' Tchaikovsky's dance, with its skirling flute over nodding bassoons and plucked strings, is cut off abruptly after a mere thirty-two bars.

d) Trepak (Russian dance). Petipa: 'At the end of the dance, Trepak with hoops. Accelerating 2/4 – 64 bars.' Tchaikovsky's dance, marked Tempo di trepak, molto vivace, is based on a Russian melodic formula familiar from Glinka's *Kamarinskaya*, or indeed the finale of his own Violin Concerto, and accelerates to its final Prestissimo through eighty-four bars.

e) Danse des mirlitons. Petipa: 'Flute dance, tempo di polacca 64–96 bars. They dance, playing reed-pipes with bubbles at their ends.' Tchaikovsky here rejects Petipa's tempo indication, and writes a gentle 2/4 Andantino that is far more in keeping with the pastoral flavour (seventy-seven bars). Familiarity should not blunt appreciation of its neatness, both in the touches of colour such as the blending of a cor anglais counterpoint with the chiming flutes and the suggestion of imitation when the violins enter, and in the deftly balanced tone colour of the brass middle section.

f) Mère Gigogne et les polichinelles. Though he followed Petipa's request for a three-part dance, 2/4 then 3/4 then 2/4, altering only the 3/4 to 6/8, and though he kept reasonably close to the numbers of bars specified, Tchaikovsky took the law into his own hands more firmly with this movement. The introduction of a character from French fairy tale (the Old Woman Who Lived in a Shoe) here suggested to him the use of more old French tunes. He would have known many French nursery and popular songs from childhood; his mother's French blood and the influence of his French governess Fanny Dürbach would have intensified the attraction to all things French that was normal among the *dvoryanstvo*, the Russian country-house classes. There still survives in the Davydov family in Russia (the descendants of Tchaikovsky's sister Alexandra) a beautiful edition, decorated with flower pictures, of a collection published in Paris by Plon-Nourrit as *Vieilles chansons et danses pour les petits enfants avec accompagnement de Ch. M. Widor*; and in this there is to be found 'Giroflé, girofla', the tune which makes his opening section of the movement. A second collection remaining in the Davydov family, *Chansons de France pour les petits français*, includes two others, 'Monsieur Dumollet' and 'Cadet Rousselle', of which Tchaikovsky made use. However, though these books belonged to Alexandra and her family, he was evidently fond enough of the tunes to acquire (or perhaps to have retained from childhood) a substantial collection himself, which is preserved among his books in the House-Museum at Klin. This is *Chants et chansons de France. Notices par Dumersan. Accompagnements de piano par H. Colet* (undated; but Hippolyte-Raimond Colet, a composer and teacher at the Paris Conservatoire, died in 1851, so his book would have been available in Tchaikovsky's childhood). Volume 1, subtitled 'Chants guerriers et patriotiques', includes under No. 18, 'Vive Henri IV'. Volume 3, subtitled 'Chansons choisies pour la jeunesse. Romances, rondes et complaintes', includes under No. 58, 'Cadet Rousselle' and under No. 63, 'Giroflé, girofla' ('Air composé en 1650'). The copies are not marked by Tchaikovsky, except for a note scribbled diagonally on the upper right-hand corner of the cover of the third volume:

> To be worked up:
> ~~Il était une bergère~~
> Que t'as de belles filles,
> Giroflé, girofla.

It is not known at what stage Tchaikovsky abandoned his intention of using 'Il était une bergère'; his eventual 'working-up' of 'Giroflé, girofla' keeps very close to Colet, even as to key (the tune is identical in Widor, but in F).

The growth of this by Glinka-style varied repetition makes the first section. The second, Andante, uses 'Cadet Rousselle' (quoted in Ex. 28 from Colet, but transposed from F to A, as Tchaikovsky does). The third section is a return to 'Giroflé, girofla', in a new orchestration, and ending in a faster passage.

No. 13: Waltz of the flowers

Once again, Petipa's instructions found a precise answer in

Ex.28 Andante (♩ = 72) (Orig. Allegro in Colet)

Cad - et Rous-selle a trois mais-ons, Cad-et Rous-selle a trois mais-
Qui n'ont ni pout-res, ni chev-rons, Qui n'ont ni pout-res, ni chev-

- ons, C'est pour log - er les hir - ond - el - les; Que dis - ez
- rons

vous d'Cad-et Rous - sel - le? Ah! ah! ah! mais vrai -

-ment, Cad - et Rous -selle est bon en - fant.

Tchaikovsky's imagination at the start of this famous waltz for the Sugar-Plum Fairy's attendants. He asked for 'eight bars to begin the waltz, then an extension of the bars'; Tchaikovsky responds with a four-bar woodwind phrase, answered after harp arpeggios, then answered again in a nine-bar phrase before a harp cadenza leads into the main theme. This is developed from the woodwind introduction on horns and clarinet; and the answering strain is also divided between instruments, strings and flutes with clarinets. Yet another melody follows before the main central theme, a strong, warm melody on violas and cellos whose scoring, with upper string arpeggios and off-beat woodwind and horns, also serves to provide a contrast in method. The profusion and excellence of the tunes contradict Tchaikovsky's doubts about his powers of invention, and the skill with which they are handled is comparable to anything in similar vein in his ballet music.

No. 14: Pas de deux

Since there was no possibility of Clara dancing a pas de deux with the Nutcracker Prince (Belinskaya, the original Clara, was twelve years old), there followed this suite of dances for the Sugar-Plum Fairy and Prince Orgeat. However, the opening Andante maestoso was soon given to Clara and her Prince when the former part was taken by a dancer mature enough to execute it. It is a piece in Tchaikovsky's most impassioned vein, beginning with a fervent cello theme based on a falling scale; at a *poco più mosso,* a new theme is played by the oboe and then bass clarinet, after which the music builds up to a powerful full orchestral climax out of which trombones deliver a powerful statement of the falling scale theme: it has a strong flavour of Tchaikovsky's death themes, though there is no reason why such a motive should occur here. The first ideas for his Pathetic Symphony still lay months ahead. The music is in general also close to the passionate love music of the Fifth Symphony, with its opulent scoring and emphatic climaxes. Petipa had requested that it should be 'colossal in effect'.

Variation 1. A vigorous tarantella for the male dancer.

Variation 2. For the female dancer, Tchaikovsky wrote the Dance of the Sugar Plum Fairy that has, more than any other piece of music, given the celesta a permanent place in the orchestra. Impossible he may have found it at one stage to find music for her: the discovery of the celesta stimulated him to music of the prettiness and delicacy that exactly matches her embodiment of the Kingdom of Sweets. The 'lyrical idea' upon which Tchaikovsky set so much store, it may be noted, is not here primarily melodic: the essence of the piece is the chiming chords of the celesta and the little bass clarinet half-scale that provides the surprising but ideal blend with it; and the development of the piece also depends on niceties of texture rather than of melody, including in the brief Presto that finishes the piece.

Coda. An energetic piece for both dancers, building up tension chiefly by use of scale figures.

No. 15: Final waltz and apotheosis

The entire Court join in, and the curtain falls on a final tribute to Clara.

After the charm of the Waltz of the Flowers and of the Sugar-Plum Fairy's Variation, the courtly waltz is somewhat perfunctory, expertly enough though it builds up into a climax that leads straight into the Apotheosis. Petipa asked for a 'grandiose Andante': Tchaikovsky composed a movement based on a rich scoring of the theme which had opened the act (No. 10), with shimmering strings and arpeggios on harps and celesta. A few loud chords serve to bring the curtain down.